THE
GERARD RONAY
Chocolate
Kit

BOXTREE

![MACMILLAN]

First published 1997 by Boxtree

an imprint of Macmillan Publishers Ltd
25 Eccleston Place, London SW1W 9NF
and Basingstoke

Associated companies throughout the world

ISBN 0 752 20554 4

9 8 7 6 5 4 3 2 1

A CIP catalogue record for this book is available from the British Library

The picture on page 6 from *Chocolata Inda Pusculum De qualitate & Natura Chocolatae,*
Authore Antonio Colmenero De Ledesma, Norimberg 1644 [Bodleian shelfmark 8° N.38.Med.] is reproduced
by kind permission of the Bodleian Library, University of Oxford

Design: Carole Perks
Photography: Philip Wilkins
Senior Commissioning Editor for Boxtree/Macmillan: Gordon Scott Wise
Editor: Deborah Savage

Scans and colour repro by Speedscan Ltd

Printed and bound in Italy by Manfrini S.p.a. Calliano (TN)

ACKNOWLEDGEMENTS
To thank everybody who has helped me in my pursuit of chocolate hedonism
would require a book in itself.
In the event of insufficient space to name all those without whose help I could not have
written this book, a unique mention must go to those who share my surname: my parents,
without whose support I would have had simply to make do with enjoying the works of others
rather then experiencing the ultimate accolade of bathing in the satisfaction of my own creations;
Sam, my wife, who in the face of a very cramped home swamped with chocolate showed
magnanimous patience and support; and our son Theo who, despite having started life less than
21 months previously, nevertheless displayed a highly entertaining zeal in wishing to be
gustily involved with tasting, cooking and cleaning.

THE GERARD RONAY Chocolate Kit

Contents

A Tribute to the Food of the Gods

The botanical name of the cocoa plant is
Theobroma (Greek for 'Food of the Gods') *cacao*

Presenting chocolate to the world, *c. 1640. Diana, the warrior goddess, is seen here
handing over to Neptune, the sea god, her knowledge of chocolate, so that he might
distribute it far and wide across the world.*

(Frontispiece engraving from A. Colemenero de Ledesma, Chocolata India, 1644)

Oh, venerable Chocolate!
To Your God did the Aztecs pay great homage.
In Your name were brown coloured dogs sacrificed.
And in the hope that the Gods would look kindly upon Your precious crop
Did prisoners, having taken of Your fluids,
Yield their hearts so that these would become cocoa pods.

Oh, sweet Chocolate!
To You have turned many a warrior for their strength.
In Your magic did many a suitor entrust their amorous conquests.
Upon mere sight or smell of You is many a mortal captured by Your spell,
Upon tasting does many an admirer in ecstacy swoon.

To You, oh Chocolate, I do my life decree,
Having from early infancy fallen under Your trance,
Guilty of mixing Your charm with the allure of champagne to woo my wife-to-be,
The powers, beauty and tastes of Your fruit I hereby gladly share
For others to similarly enjoy.

Introduction

Chocolate is not merely an inanimate food. Festooned in history, entrenched into many a society, unique in its chemical composition and seductive in smell and taste, this creation of nature has a personality all of its own. I myself am unashamedly dedicated to acquainting myself with all sides of its character, and it is with great joy that I take this opportunity to share my knowledge and passion.

To cook with chocolate is just one way to discover its enchanting qualities, but one that I have spent years exploring. The recipes in this book are a testimony to the flexibility of chocolate, for as you will discover it can be combined with flavours your imagination might never have considered, with mouth-watering results.

Further testing of your imagination is the ease with which chocolate can be elevated to the prestigious world of art. With my step-by-step instructions and the moulds accompanying this book, you will be able to create works which can be indefinitely admired - that is, until the visual senses have been edifyingly rewarded, at which point your gustatory senses can be given ample reward for their patient wait.

The approach that I have adopted throughout is, if I may hijack a term from the world of computer vernacularism, 'user-friendly'. Instructions and explanations have been geared towards both the newcomer to the practical side of chocolate as well as to the expert. Alternatives are given, making allowances for varying levels of equipment or facilities. And to round this all off, I have compiled a list of useful addresses and contacts to assist you in the search for further equipment or advice.

Implicit in this book is my belief that life is there to be enjoyed. So amongst all the recipes and instructions you will find anecdotes, historical, scientific or personal in nature, all designed to make the task in hand as fun, rewarding and as interesting as possible.

GERARD RONAY
Chocolate Maker

Chapter 1

The chocolate labyrinth

What is chocolate?

You are at a dinner party. You want to liven up the debate. The familiar menu of politics-religion-sport springs to mind. Stop there! Try my favourite trump card - talk chocolate!

Give most people an opportunity to talk about chocolate and the range of responses can be as telling as the psychometric 'ink-blot' test. Some, at the mere invitation to share their passion for chocolate, spontaneously but unknowingly betray how they might appear in the height of orgasm! Some subconsciously reveal their opinion of their own body image, with comments such as 'Aagh! Chocolate is too fattening', or 'Ugh! You can get acne from eating chocolate, can't you?' Some may relish talking about their addiction: 'That's nothing. Yesterday I had two (five, ten...) chocolate bars...'. Others may betray a tendency towards fastidiousness: 'Johnny made such a mess with his chocolate ice cream that he is never

getting it again!' There are also those who will tell you their doctors have forbidden them chocolate but then, probably in the same breath, display a rebellious streak: 'I won't tell my doctor if you won't'. And then there are those who are itching to talk politics and will use chocolate as an example of those European bureaucrats interfering yet again: 'How dare they say our chocolate shouldn't be called chocolate!'

Similarly, each person's concept of what chocolate is can be equally diverse, just as psychologists assure us that the way we perceive, say, the colour red differs from individual to individual. At the end of the day, it is your taste buds that are the most important, not anybody else's. It is not my intention to dictate what you should like but to assist you in tying up your expectations with what is actually available and to give you the opportunity to explore what might be new combinations of flavours.

Chocolate fundamentals: (clockwise, from top) milk, cocoa powder, cocoa beans, sugar, vanilla, colourings and soya beans (the source of lecithin which, like the egg yolk in mayonnaise, encourages the individual components to remain homogenous and not to separate) and cocoa butter. In different proportions according to type, the spectrum of basic forms of chocolate will include a selection from these ingredients.

A guide to the basic forms of chocolate

Legal jargon aside (for there is, needless to say, a complex definition buried within UK legislation), I find the following visualisation useful: imagine splitting the edible part of an already roasted cocoa bean into two main components: its own natural fat (in other words, cocoa butter), and a brown, tarry sludge.

Now imagine savouring a piece of your favourite chocolate: after you have lustfully inhaled its aroma, the chocolate in your mouth teasingly takes its time to release its rich, comforting flavour, which blissfully lingers even when the final morsel is well on its way down your digestive tract. It is to cocoa butter and its property of melting at just below body temperature that a great deal of this pleasure is due. As the heat is absorbed from the roof of your mouth to melt the cocoa butter, your senses relay this back to your brain as a positive sensation. Hence, if you try the same chocolate both solid or molten, you will find the two forms score differently in the pleasure stakes.

Returning to my figurative lump of 'brown sludge', this is where most of the characteristic flavour of chocolate is housed. How this sludge is processed, along with what becomes of the cocoa butter, will determine the format of the chocolate as well as (ideally, but, confusingly not always) the packaging label.

PLAIN/DARK *COUVERTURE*

Content: 'sludge' + cocoa butter + sugar + tiny amounts of vanilla/vanillin + lecithin (an emulsifier)

This is what I regard as the purest form of eating chocolate. The term *couverture* implies to the trade a high level of cocoa butter, which, consequently, means that it will be easier to use for coating.

❖ This is the best type for coating and is also excellent for eating and cooking. But beware, a high level of cocoa solids (as this automatically has) does not necessarily imply good quality (in fact, I have been known to spit out certain unpalatable versions), so I advise you, if possible, to taste before purchasing.

❖ It is easily obtainable from most professional food suppliers as *couverture* (for sources, please refer to the directory).

❖ It can also be found in some high-quality delicatessens or chocolate boutiques as well as supermarkets although in these outlets it is unlikely to be known as *couverture*. Instead, confusingly, it will be sold as 'cooking' or 'baking' chocolate or even simply as 'eating' chocolate. If there is nobody around who can help you, you can use your search for *couverture* as a legitimate excuse for munching your way through several bars! Or you might get some clues from the ingredients label: go for cocoa solids higher than 50 per cent but reconsider if the chocolate flavour has been boosted with cocoa powder (this is likely to be fine for cooking and for chocolate centres but would be too strong and bitter for using in coatings).

❖ The shelf life, from the point of view of being palatable, is almost irrelevant, especially if the chocolate has been kept in the right conditions. Cocoa butter can last for some time (years), and the absence of milk products in dark *couverture* means that there are no other components that can go rancid. However, the actual taste of chocolate can, like wine, change with time: in fact, with high-quality chocolate, the taste improves with ageing for a while before it starts to deteriorate.

❖ *Couverture* does not (yet!) attract VAT, unlike some other versions of chocolate, a curious anomaly when VAT is added to luxury/non-essential items. I can only assume that nobody in HM Customs & Excise responsible for classifying products appreciates fine chocolate enough to realise that this type of cooking chocolate can also make the best eating version!

❖ Sometimes, especially if buying from a catering supplier, you might be faced with the choice of buttons (technically known as *pistoles*) versus tablet or bar. Buttons tend to be more expensive but, at the

same time, are more convenient, especially if you need to melt your chocolate quickly, or for cooling chocolate when small amounts of solid chocolate are added to warm, molten chocolate (see page 26).

❖ Weight for weight, *couverture* is more expensive than other types (cocoa butter is a relatively very expensive component of chocolate) but the availability of *couverture* in large blocks can bring the price down significantly.

❖ *Couverture* can be used in others' recipes but if butter is also included in the recipe, I would advise reducing the suggested amount of butter slightly, allowing for the high cocoa-butter-content of *couverture*.

MILK *COUVERTURE*
Content: as for plain *couverture* + milk

I have heard some chocolate purists proclaim that any version other than plain or dark chocolate is simply not chocolate. Rubbish! I love milk chocolate as much as dark, whilst admitting that milk and plain are two totally individual personalities, which come into their own in very different circumstances. For me 'milk' is equivalent to cosily wrapping up in a duvet on a cold English winter evening, with a log fire crackling in the background. 'Plain' conjures up the image of touching soft, freshly washed and ironed bed sheets, a wonderful tactile and aromatic experience after an exhausting and sweaty day's work.

Many a time has milk chocolate cossetted me after a particularly harrassing experience, whilst dark chocolate has rounded off many a memorable gastronomic feast.

My general comments relating to plain *couverture* also apply to the milk variety, however discrepancies in overall flavour are increased in the case of the latter by the form of the milk added. Continental manufacturers tend towards simply adding milk powder, whereas the English, in the main, use milk that has been condensed with sugar and some chocolate, giving a distinctive boiled-milk flavour to the chocolate. At the end of the day, the choice is down to your preference.

BAKING/COOKING CHOCOLATE

This is where confusion can set in, for this term cannot be found in UK legislation and yet it is readily used in labelling, especially in chocolate sold to the public.

In some cases, the term implies high quality, for, to achieve a concentrated chocolate taste, the proportion of cocoa solids will probably be higher than it would be in what is regarded as standard eating chocolate. In fact, as has already been mentioned, 'cooking chocolate' might even be *couverture* in disguise - although it may not be clear from the wrapper.

If so, it is ideal for both coating and for the centres in this book.

In other cases, 'cooking chocolate', especially the American version, often implies a rougher, less refined chocolate. It is, not surprisingly, suitable for cooking with and for my centres, but not as pleasurable for eating (in fact, sometimes distinctly displeasing!) and, therefore, I would steer away from this version when it comes to coating or for moulds.

Confounded? Yet again, the solution is to ask (if you are in a specialist shop) and/or taste.

EATING CHOCOLATE

Content: 'sludge' + cocoa butter + (probably) a cocoa butter substitute, such as vegetable fat, replacing some cocoa butter which might have been removed + sugar + vanilla/vanillin + lecithin

This is where I encroach upon a minefield of controversy: it is for this version of chocolate that European legislators have endeavoured to ban the use of the term 'chocolate', on the grounds that other European countries do not use cocoa-butter substitutes. Flying my white flag of neutrality, I would have to say that it is down to your preference as to whether you like this version; here, however, are my findings regarding using it for the purposes of this book:

❖ Since the proportion of cocoa butter can determine the fluidity of chocolate when molten, eating chocolate with less cocoa butter than *couverture* is more difficult to use for cooking and coating, but not impossible.

❖ When cocoa butter solidifies, unlike water, it shrinks. This is an important property when it comes to using moulds. As the chocolate hardens, it should break away cleanly from the surface of the mould, so that your creation should need no coercion to part company with its mould. The 'shrinkability' of eating chocolate is consequently less than that for *couverture*, but, nevertheless, with a little bit more patience it can be used for moulding work.

❖ The low level of cocoa solids in eating chocolate will mean that the strength of the chocolate taste (as imparted by what I have called chocolate 'sludge') will be less. If you use this chocolate for my recipes, you may wish to boost the flavour by adding a small amount of cocoa powder (a tablespoon or two for each batch).

❖ It is this chocolate that attracts the attention of the VAT office, given away by its presence in the confectionery section as opposed to the cookery department.

WHITE CHOCOLATE

Content: as for milk chocolate, but no 'sludge'

The real aficionado of bitter chocolate might frown upon this version, for the component that is responsible for the taste of chocolate is totally absent. But for those (myself included) who unashamedly go into raptures over the soothing mixture of cream and sugar, what better partner to wed it with than cocoa butter, conveniently solid at room temperature but so comforting as it melts and dissolves in your mouth! Besides, my allegiance to white chocolate was developed during my childhood, when I fancied myself as an exact look-alike of the enviable Milky Bar kid (notwithstanding the absence of glasses), as I proclaimed that all the bars were on me. Sadly, I had to wait a long time before I could turn fantasy into reality as an adult!

❖ The term *couverture*, strangely enough, does not exist for white chocolate. However, the variation in taste and texture in different kinds of white chocolate is not so great as in plain, so you might well be happy with any form of white chocolate.

❖ Due to its relatively high proportion of milk products, white chocolate is more likely to develop a rancid taste than dark chocolate; nevertheless, it still has a shelf-life of many months.

❖ Be warned: of the three main types of chocolate, white is the hardest to use, since it is less forgiving than plain and milk chocolate if you get the temperatures for heating and cooling wrong.

COLOURED CHOCOLATE

Content: as for white chocolate, but with food colouring(s) and occasionally, extra flavourings such as orange flavouring for orange chocolate

With the addition of coloured chocolate to your painting palette, the world of chocolate art in your hands becomes infinite! Coloured chocolate will almost invariably impress even though, tacitly, you might feel that the end result is a far cry from your original intention (some of my best designs were complete mistakes). There are three possible sources of coloured chocolate.

❖ Coloured *couverture* is normally only available from specialist suppliers to the trade (a list of these can be found in the Directory on page 61); consequently it comes in large units (such as 5 kg blocks). If you, along with others in your area, were to start a chocolate-art revolution, you might be able to persuade your local chocolate specialist to buy in this chocolate and sell it to you in smaller quantities.

❖ Fat-soluble colouring (available from specialist stockists for mail-order; please refer to page 61) is a very effective way of producing exactly the colour you

want in small amounts, by mixing it with white chocolate, which you can get almost anywhere. By buying, say, three different colours, and by mixing the pigments when the chocolate is molten, you can achieve almost all the colours in the rainbow for a relatively modest cost.

❖ Food colouring for sugar/marzipan work can be found in almost any well stocked shop or supermarket. The problem with these is that they contain very small amounts of water, which will adversely affect the consistency of the chocolate, possibly rendering it unworkable. I would, therefore, advise going for either of

the two previous options, if you can. If you can't, by all means use these water-based pigments but in very small amounts (a drop at a time) and accept that you will not be able to obtain bold colours (trying to do so will ruin your chocolate).

COCOA MASS
Content: 'sludge' + cocoa butter (i.e. no sugar)

This is the real thing: 100 per cent chocolate. Pedantically, according to British legislation, it cannot be called chocolate, since it does not contain sugar! You might have to shop around for cocoa mass but it can be found in specialist delicatessens or chocolate shops. Go easy with this - it is like raw chilli. I have known people who could not spit it out fast enough. Moreover, it can temporarily knock out your ability to taste, yet alone enjoy, any other foods. Since it looks like any other plain chocolate, leave a small morsel in a very tempting place, and I can guarantee that your chocolate stock will henceforth be safe from any chocolate marauders, without your having to confront them!

❖ It's great, when used in small amounts, for cooking (but not for coating), in order to obtain a punchy chocolate flavour without resorting to cocoa powder, with its characteristic, acidic taste.

COCOA POWDER
Content: 'sludge' (i.e. very little or no cocoa butter)

One of my greatest pleasures in life is to find a bag of very refined cocoa powder (normally stocked by suppliers to the catering profession), to get my nose as close as possible to the cocoa, and to sniff. Ecstasy! (Afterwards, you are advised to inspect your nose in the mirror before showing your face to the public!)

Cocoa powder is the closest to the form in which chocolate was consumed before the Europeans discovered it in the seventeenth century, when the Aztecs were

mixing chocolate with hot spices and taking it as a drink. It would have been oilier than we know drinking chocolate today, since the technique of separating out cocoa butter is a relatively modern phenomenon (it was discovered at the end of the nineteenth century and is a process known as 'Dutching'; no reward for guessing where it was discovered).

In addition to its familiar uses for drinking and for baking, cocoa powder is an essential item for the chocolate-making store cupboard. This is shown by the proliferation of cocoa-dusted truffles, for the following reasons:

❖ The finished product, when covered in cocoa powder, is more durable, so it's easier to transport (chocolates without cocoa powder are very prone to showing finger prints and to scuffing).

❖ The attractive finish of cocoa powder can helpfully conceal a chocolate coating that looks whitish, dull or even stale, otherwise technically known as having 'bloomed' ('sugar bloom' is explained on page 57, whilst 'fat bloom' is discussed on page 58). So you do not have to be the world's finest chocolatier to produce chocolates that you can be proud of!

❖ Its distinct flavour is liked by many but is also frowned upon by some because of its bitter taste, as well as its propensity to increase your laundry bill. Nevertheless, I find a cocoa powder coating very useful as a contrast to a very sweet centre.

Type of chocolate	Taste	Uses
Couverture	Can be the best to eat, but beware of being too bitter. For milk variety, taste will vary according to form of milk added	Cooking, eating and coating (depending on taste)
Baking/Cooking	Will vary widely: may equally be *couverture* or very unrefined	Not recommended for coating and eating unless *couverture* in disguise. Fine for cooking
Eating	Less strong taste (lower level of cocoa solids) May need to boost with cocoa for recipes	OK for cooking. Can be used for mould-work but other types better
White	Not traditional 'chocolate', as it contains no cocoa solids; creamy and sweet	Harder to work with than dark or milk, but useful for contrasting tones in decorative work
Coloured	As white chocolate, unless specific flavours added	Available ready-made for decorative work. Alternatively, use fat-soluble pigments added to white chocolate
Cocoa mass	Very bitter, if not unpalatable, if eaten on its own	In cooking, use in small amounts to boost taste instead of cocoa powder
Cocoa powder	Dry and bitter	Boosting flavour (although acidic in taste); coating sweet-centred truffles; disguising imperfectly tempered chocolate

Chapter 2

Keeping your temper
Tempering chocolate

Imagine yourself as a parent. Whilst your child is away you dare to ignore the 'KEEP OUT' sign on his (I shall use 'his' instead of 'her', since in my life 'his' is reality) door and enter his territory. It's a tip! Despite all the patience you have cultivated in your role as a parent, this pigsty is intolerable. You tidy up, ignoring the common sense that tells you it will not be long after your child's return before he re-exerts his authority. Nevertheless, there is something curiously rewarding in knowing, for a short time, at least, that your child's room is looking pristine.

Chocolate is your child's bedroom! If you want molten chocolate to set with a sheen that you will be proud to show off (such as for mould work or for coating), the individual elements or molecules need to be arranged, when the chocolate is molten, into a structured, uniform order. As in your child's bedroom, this is unlikely to happen of its own accord: chocolate left to its own devices will set in a variegated form - globular and oily in places, mottled and grey in others, or even shiny in the odd spot. To introduce order into your chocolate, it needs to be 'tempered', which means cooling your chocolate to a precise temperature, followed immediately by reheating very slightly. You might hear that mastering this technique can be a real effort. However, the following tips are intended to make it as easy as possible, no matter with what equipment and space your working area is endowed.

There are occasions when it is not important whether your chocolate sets with a sheen or not (for example, in cooking or in my recipes for fillings), in which case I am sure you will need no further encouragement to leap past this introduction to tempering and go straight to the recipes (page 45).

Temper-free fun with tempered chocolate!

Tempering basics

There are three main stages for tempering: melting, cooling and slightly reheating.

Melting chocolate

All the soluble components of chocolate (such as cocoa butter and sugar) are melted during heating. However it is important not to exceed maximum temperatures; doing so will destroy the molecular structures, the possibility of a perfect finish, and even the taste. Stick to these temperatures and your chocolate is even safe for children to handle, since, at these heat levels, there is no danger from burning. The maximum temperatures vary according to the type of chocolate (generally, the greater the proportion of sugar and milk products in relation to what I have hitherto referred to as 'sludge', the lower will be the temperature at which all the various molecules organise themselves). As a rule of thumb, the temperatures drop by 2°C as one goes from plain to milk to white.

I usually heat plain chocolate to around 45°C but, in some cases, such as where there is a high proportion of cocoa butter, it can be taken to over 50°C (this will normally be confirmed by the instructions on the packaging). Milk chocolate should be taken to around 43°C and white chocolate should not be taken above 40°C. A sign that the chocolate has been overheated, damaging the structure of some molecules, is that the molten chocolate is thicker than normal and may even be gritty or lumpy. If this happens, try sieving the chocolate or adding some new chocolate.

Cooling

At a specific temperature, if the chocolate has been stirred regularly, the structure of the molecules will be as close as possible to a uniform structure. However, at this stage, the chocolate will probably be too thick and lumpy to work with. For plain chocolate this temperature is around 27°C, for milk chocolate 25°C and for white chocolate 23°C .

RECOMMENDED TEMPERATURES FOR TEMPERING CHOCOLATE			
TYPE	HEATING	COOLING	REHEATING
Plain chocolate	42-45°C	26-28°C	30-31°C
Milk chocolate	41-43°C	24-26°C	28-29°C
White chocolate	38-40°C	22-24°C	26-27°C

Reheating

The final stage is to reheat the chocolate slightly, by 3-4°C. The chocolate should now be fluid enough to use, whilst the individual molecules should remain in their most stable form. Wander slightly above this temperature and you may well have to start all over again but not necessarily! (I will return to this later, on page 26.)

Far left: *Fat, or cocoa-butter, bloom occurs as chocolate re-sets after exposure to heat, or when the chocolate hasn't been tempered properly.* Inside left and inside right: *This whiteness can occur when chocolate is exposed to moisture, whereby the sugar content recrystallizes, which can occur when removing chocolate suddenly from a cold environment into a hot one (e.g. from cold fridge to warm kitchen).* Below: *Perfect!*

Ways to measure the temperature of chocolate

Thermometer

When melting chocolate for the first time, using a thermometer could be the easiest way, be it an extravagant digital affair or a glass thermometer (provided it is sensitive between 20 and 55°C). However, when using a thermometer for cooling, regularly check that no chocolate has set around the bulb or probe, which might give a false reading (because this set chocolate would be cooler than the batch as a whole). Remember that every thermometer is different, so that the readings yours gives may be slightly out, although the difference registered between heated and cooled chocolate will be accurate. At the end of the day, the most reliable thermometer (once it has been finely tuned!), which you can take anywhere, is yourself; so I suggest that you try to master one of the following techniques.

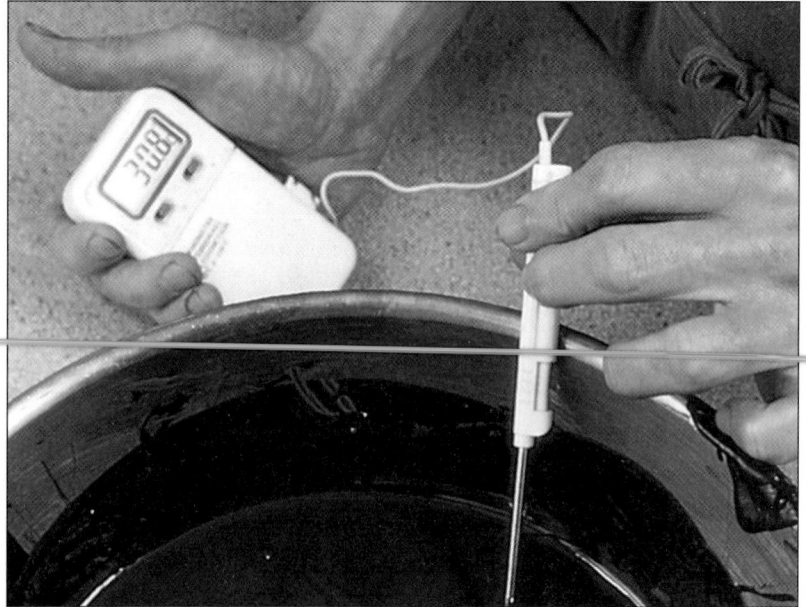

Fingers

These are not quite as accurate as your lips (see opposite), for the fingers are not as sensitive, but the same principles apply. Instead of dipping a finger in the chocolate, you might wish to try a more hygiene-conscious method: feeling the outside of the bowl of chocolate, and thereby gauging the temperature, a method I find effective when trying to maintain already-tempered chocolate at the right temperature.

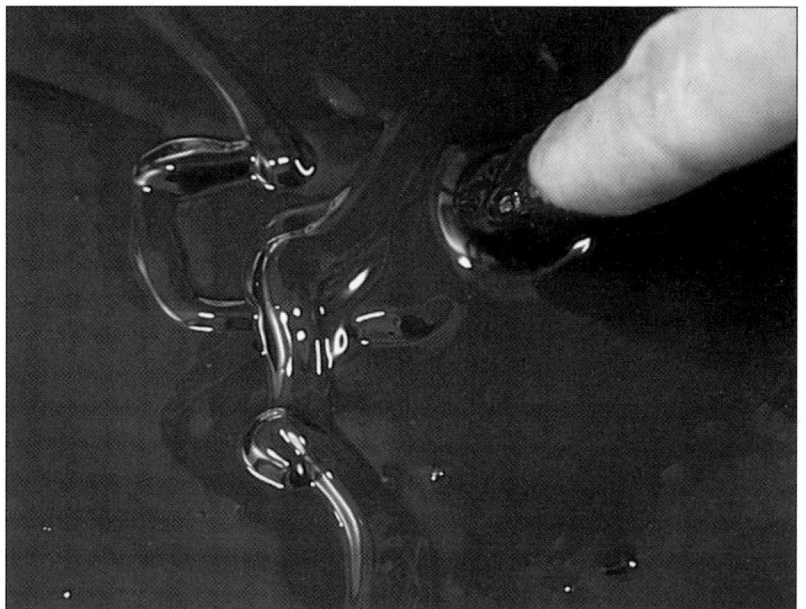

Lips

This is a wonderful method if you are a chocoholic but not to be attempted if you are out to impress the environmental health officer! The rationale behind this technique is that the lips are one of the most sensitive parts of the body and also tend to be at your body's core temperature (unlike your hands, for example, which can often be colder). Since chocolate involves temperatures not far from body temperature, which is around 37°C, one can fairly accurately gauge the temperature, although it may take a little practice (and many a false moustache of chocolate!).

Before testing, stir your chocolate well and then, from the middle of your batch and using the back of a spoon, quickly bring a small amount of chocolate up to your top lip. At about 43-45°C (the temperature up to which plain and milk chocolate can be heated), the chocolate should register as very warm: if it hurts or burns, you have gone too far! 26°C (the lowest temperature for cooling plain chocolate) is positively cool. 30-31°C (the temperature at which to keep plain chocolate tempered) should register as tepid.

But beware, you might have to tweak your personal thermometer readings, if your own body temperatures are out of line (that is, if you are feeling unusually hot or cold).

Sight

Master this technique and you might well feel that you are living and understanding chocolate. Besides, for those whose memory is not very retentive of numbers, this saves having to remember all those temperatures! Provided that you have heated your chocolate gently, once the batch has totally melted, you should find that it is pretty close to the ideal maximum temperature. At the other end of the scale, during cooling, when, on stirring, it starts thickening or becoming lumpy, as if making a roux or real custard, you have arrived at the lowest temperature. Heat slightly whilst stirring frequently, until the lumps have almost disappeared, and your chocolate should be perfectly tempered.

The best ways to heat and melt chocolate

Ideally, the chocolate should be broken up into as small pieces as feasible, achieved by either: cutting with a large, sharp knife; using a hammer (a hammer is a standard piece of equipment for me, as is a hairdryer, about which you will read later!); dropping on the floor (having beforehand wrapped your block in a bag or clingfilm); or simply using chocolate buttons/pistoles (see page 10). This way, the process will take less time and, moreover, the risk of overheating the chocolate is minimised.

The quantity of chocolate obviously depends on how much you will need but, since chocolate is reusable, it is better to be on the generous side the larger the quantity, the easier it is to control the temperatures and, therefore, to temper the chocolate. There should be a healthy amount of chocolate (about two-thirds) relative to the size of the bowl. On the other hand, resist the urge to be too generous: overfilling the bowl can turn out to be a frustratingly mucky affair!

Tempering kettle

If you have a few thousand pounds to spare as well as a few thousand chocolates to make, this is a wonderful machine that does it all for you automatically (the equivalent to the luxury of a dishwasher). But, in its absence, one of the following should suffice!

Bain-marie

In other words, a bowl, pan or other receptacle within another pan. These are readily available, or you could buy a double saucepan, but a cheaper version is an easy DIY job. From your own stock of bowls (metal or ceramic) and saucepans, find a bowl and saucepan of diameters such that the rim of the bowl sits on the top of the pan (so that very little steam or heat escapes) and of depths such that the bottom of the bowl is not in direct contact with the pan. Although you might think it is easy to melt chocolate, there are, in fact, some common problems. The tips (below) should ensure that you do not run into them.

TIPS FOR USING A BAIN-MARIE

❖ *The amount of water you put in the saucepan depends on whether you intend to use water at 100°C or around 80°C (for example, out of a recently boiled kettle or from the tap). If the water is boiling (that is, the saucepan is being continuously heated), it is important that it does not come in contact with the bottom of the bowl of chocolate: it could ruin the chocolate by overheating. To avoid this risk (especially if you are liable to be distracted by phone calls or inquisitive friends or family), my preference is for using water that is hot, as opposed to boiling, for then it is not so essential to ensure the bowl sits out of the water. If the chocolate does not melt with the first batch of water, simply replace your cooled water with more hot water.*

❖ *Stir the chocolate regularly. Start by stirring from around the outside of the bowl, bringing your chocolate into the centre of the bowl; the frequency is determined by the ferocity of the heat. If the water is boiling, stir it every minute or two; if it is not boiling, every five minutes should suffice.*

❖ *The marriage of water with chocolate will produce a very strange relationship! Even a very small amount of water will affect the molecular structure of the whole batch of chocolate, rendering it unusable (except as an alternative to Polyfilla: water irreversibly turns chocolate into a thick paste!). It is, therefore, important to ensure that all equipment is totally dry, especially if using wooden spoons.*

Microwave

Some sources advise against this method but, provided that you proceed gently and cautiously, ignore this advice. The microwave is my preferred technique (especially if patience or time is limited and you need to melt large, solid blocks of chocolate).

It is crucial to avoid burning your chocolate: it's pungent and lingering smell and taste is easily identifiable and unforgivingly unpleasant. If you have burnt your chocolate, discard the whole batch immediately, since the burnt taste will permeate the molten chocolate, even if only a small part was affected originally. You will be sensibly erring on the side of caution if you cook on medium power for a minute at a time.

Don't be disconsolate if your chocolate appears reluctant to start melting; it may stay solid for some time but, when it visibly starts to melt, it will do so suprisingly quickly. When able to stir, do so after each burst of heating (I hope you have remembered not to use a steel bowl!).

Professional bain-marie

Your own construction

Oven

This can be either a purpose-made or ordinary domestic oven. With a purpose-designed oven you should be able to set the oven at around 40°C and then safely leave your chocolate overnight, knowing that, next day, it will be ready and willing to be tempered! The domestic oven could be a different story: it is best to experiment with a small amount of chocolate, setting the oven at its lowest temperature, before you commit yourself to a large batch. But if you place your chocolate away from the source of heat, this can be very successful, freeing you from the stove for an hour or two whilst you get on with other tasks. Do remember to go back to check and stir every ten minutes or so.

Directly over the heat source

Aware that my audacity in including this method may bring yelps of horror from some of my professional colleagues, I will, nevertheless, recommend this method, provided that:

❖ You only use this method for small amounts of chocolate;

❖ You break the chocolate into small pieces beforehand;

❖ You are in a rush (but still have your wits about you);

❖ You stir the chocolate continuously throughout; and

❖ You only leave your saucepan or bowl on or close to the heat for short periods at a time (say, a few seconds) and then remove it from the heat for, say, double the time. Rotate the bowl each cycle so that, each time, a different part is in direct contact with the heat.

Techniques for cooling the chocolate

Now that the chocolate has been heated to the temperature at which all the cocoa butter molecules of different shapes have melted, when cooling they should be encouraged to recrystallize into one specific form. Here follow several alternative methods for this stage in the tempering process, but in all it is important that the chocolate is stirred often to discourage the formation of unwelcome molecular structures, and that no moisture or, for that matter, foreign particles, should be allowed to intrude.

Using a marble table or slab

In professional circles this is normally the first method to be mastered, since it allows rapid and sometimes dramatic familiarisation with how chocolate cools. As the chocolate runs over the surface, throwing up its seductive aromas, it can also be a breathtaking and mouthwatering spectacle. But beware, don't wear your best shoes: my first attempt saw more chocolate ending up on the floor than in the bowl, much to the choleric dismay of my Gallic mentor! Less glamorous, but more easily-mastered methods are detailed on page 26.

I Pour about three-quarters of your warm chocolate on to the surface, leaving the remaining untempered quarter in the bowl.

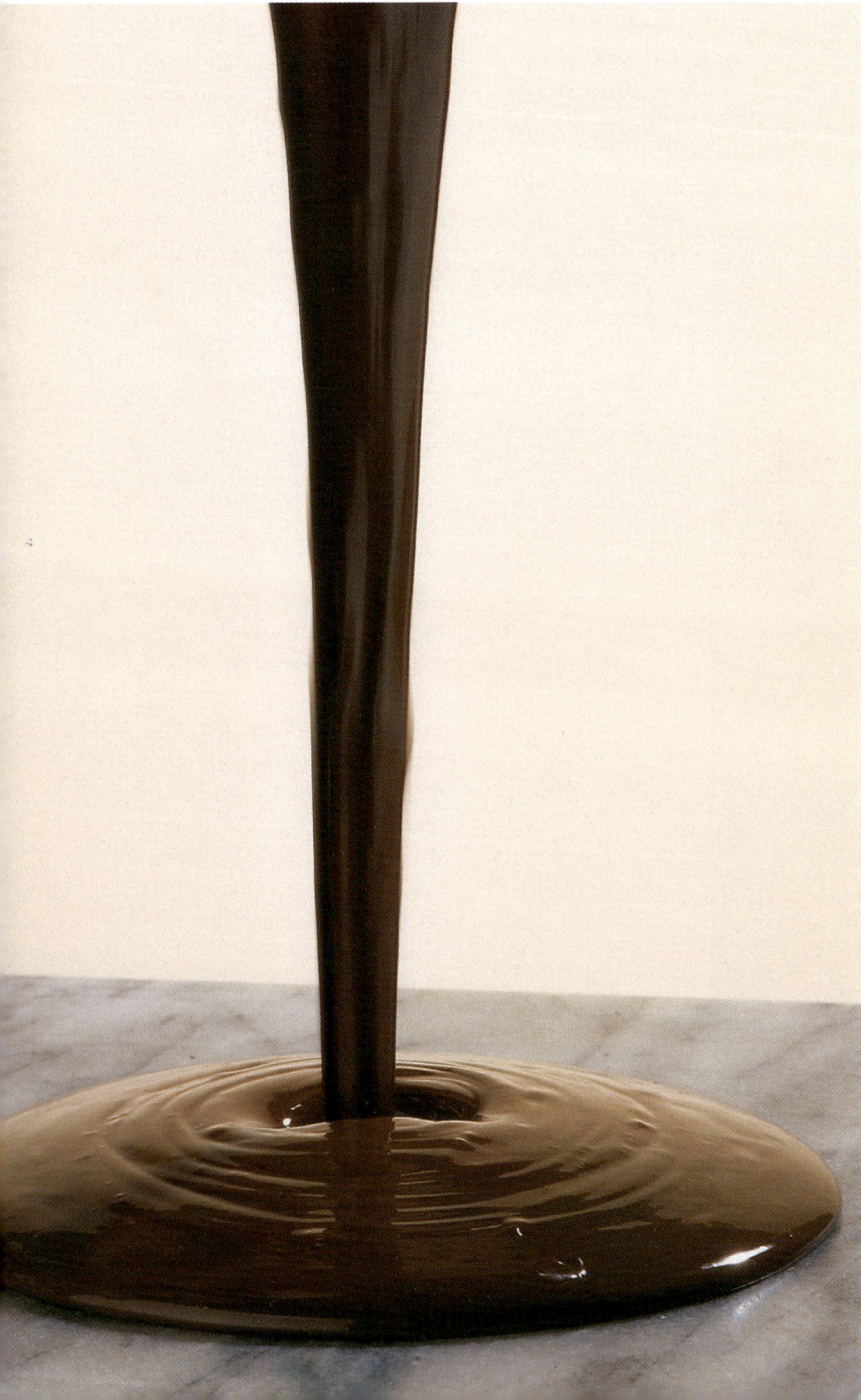

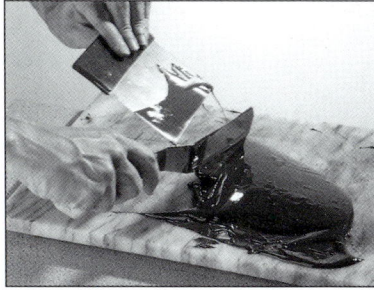

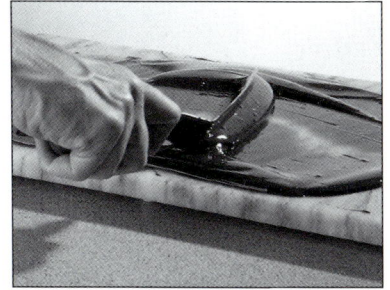

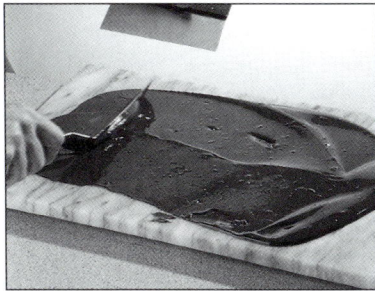

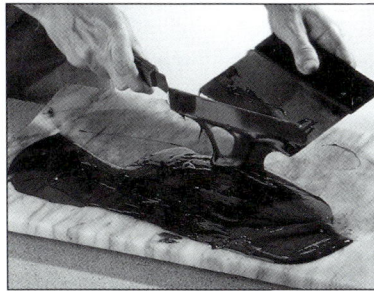

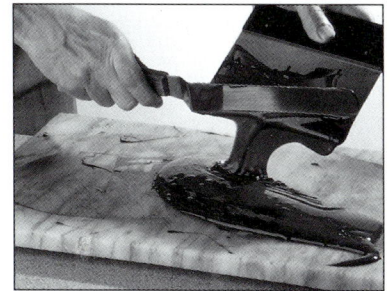

2 Using two scrapers or palette knives, spread the pool of chocolate over the surface as thinly as possible.

3 Gather up the chocolate into the smallest pool possible.

4 Repeat the process, until the texture starts to thicken.

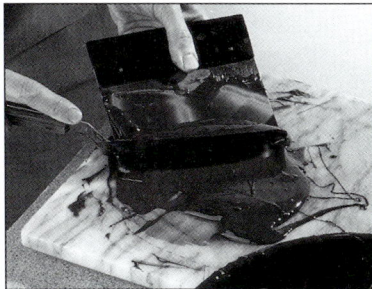

5 Quickly (but calmly!) scrape up all the chocolate and put it back in the same bowl, which still contains some warm chocolate (there is a technique for transferring the chocolate but you will acquire it through trial and error, as well as a lot of finger-licking!).

6 Mix the cold and warm chocolate thoroughly and, if fate is on your side, you might have achieved at first attempt a perfectly tempered bowl of chocolate (see page 26) and a well-earned opportunity to relax. If you do not succeed the first time, repeat the above process, pouring out a smaller amount of chocolate. You will get there in the end.

SECRETS FOR SUCCESS

The room temperature needs to be at most 21°C and humidity levels should be as low as possible (in other words, as steam-free an atmosphere as possible).

A large, dry, clutter-free, flat surface: marble is the best material, since it retains its heat, or rather coolness, for a relatively long time, but a stainless steel table top could also serve. The dimensions required will, obviously, depend on the amount of chocolate that is going to be poured on to it; remember that even a small amount of chocolate can run far.

Two metal 'scrapers' (or metal triangles such as a mason's tool) or two palette knives (from a kitchenware specialist) or a combination of these.

An interruption-free environment. Removing a large pool of chocolate that has solidified due to a moment's distraction is not an easy or enviable task!

Clothing devoid of cat or dog hairs, preferably with sleeves rolled up.

No flying insects. Molten chocolate is a very effective fly-killer!

The following ways of cooling chocolate can be equally effective, but less messy:

Adding chocolate buttons Add finely chopped pieces or buttons of solid chocolate to your bowl of heated chocolate and stir continuously. You will find that, as the pieces melt, the temperature of your chocolate will be brought down relatively rapidly. The proportion of solid chocolate to molten should be in the region of one part to four, but add it bit by bit.

Sink of cold water Good method for fairly rapid and well controlled cooling. Partly fill the sink with water from the cold tap, so it will come half to two-thirds of the way up the bowl. You will need to stir (again, from the outside inwards) frequently (every couple of minutes). However, you are dealing with one of chocolate's worst enemies: water. Take extra care to ensure that splashing is kept to a minimum (get a plumber to repair your dripping tap).

Refrigerator This is a technique I use when I'm in a hurry but, at the same time, have other things to do. However, it is like using the microwave for heating chocolate; the transition from one stage to another (in this case, from molten to solid) can take you by surprise. It is best to check the chocolate in the refrigerator frequently (every 1 to 3 minutes) and to stir each time.

Room temperature This is a technique I learnt myself and I find it extremely effective, especially when there are other tasks to perform; the chocolate is on its way to being tempered with the minimum of attention having to be paid. Simply leave your chocolate on the sideboard to cool, stirring every five to ten minutes. The cooler your room (ideally, 18-20°C), the more effective (and faster) will be the process; this is not recommended during a heatwave!

Reheating

Once the chocolate has cooled, you need to reheat it by a few degrees (2-3°C), to make it workable. Set about this with a minimum of delay, once the chocolate has cooled down to the required temperature. If you don't it will take more than just a few degrees of heating to re-melt your bowl of solidified chocolate!

The same methods suggested for melting chocolate are all appropriate but, obviously, the process here has to be much shorter: the microwave should be set at medium for 5-10 seconds at a time; the water in your bain-marie should be hot but not boiling; and, if you use direct heat, be very, very careful. I would avoid using the oven for reheating, since the temperature control is too imprecise (unless you are using a purpose-designed warming device for chocolate, which permits finer tuning). Alternatively, you may wish to try adding a small amount of warm, untempered chocolate (if you still have room in the bowl), until it reaches the required temperature. You still, of course, need to stir continuously.

The temper test:
how to tell if the chocolate is tempered properly

This is it (or not, in which case, anybody in firing range is advised to flee rapidly)! Stir your chocolate and take out a small amount from the middle. Then allow some of this chocolate to drop on to a flat surface such as a palette knife, ordinary knife, or small piece of greaseproof paper or baking parchment. Put it aside somewhere cool (less than 20°C) and leave to set. If your chocolate is properly tempered, it should start to set fairly rapidly; the process may be apparent within a minute (plain chocolate tends to set slightly faster than milk or white, and it is also easier to observe the changes in it). Once set, it should appear like brand-new chocolate: shiny and devoid of streaks or dull patches. Bad- or off-tempered chocolate will take considerably longer to set and will appear mottled, grey and old (under microscopic magnification, you would see that the cocoa butter molecules exist in a variety of forms, as opposed to tempered chocolate, in which one particular molecular form predominates). It might well taste stale, because this is how the brain interprets the longer, uneven process of the untempered chocolate melting in your mouth; the different forms of the cocoa butter molecules melt at different temperatures). If you break it, it won't snap as cleanly or easily as well tempered chocolate.

KEEPING YOUR CHOCOLATE TEMPERED

You need to keep tempered chocolate at a constant temperature. Conveniently, there is a small range of temperatures (1-3°C) which your tempered chocolate can tolerate, so it is not essential to maintain exactly the same temperature all the time. In fact, the ideal temperature will change according to how long it has been tempered for, but this you will learn to recognise and control with practice.

***Bain-marie** In the absence of specialist equipment with in-built thermostats, this is my preferred method. By keeping your water warm to tepid, you can get fine control for a relatively long period of time. (see illustration on page 23).*

***Microwave** When the chocolate starts to become lumpy or too thick to work with stick it in the microwave but for just a few seconds at a time, on medium power.*

***Direct heat** As always, be extra-vigilant not to overheat!*

***Oven** This is my least favourite method: the temperature control is too imprecise.*

***Room temperature** Working in a heatwave (up to 28°C) is not recommended but, with clever use of a refrigerator, it is possible. But beware, don't allow any sweat to drop into your chocolate.!*

If tempering goes wrong
If you don't succeed, don't despair!

There are ways around tempering and, besides, there are a couple of things you can do which may rescue the situation.

Cocoa powder Cocoa powder is excellent for using when coating chocolates made with off-tempered chocolate. The attractive matt coating hides the fact that the chocolate isn't very shiny.

Moulds can be very forgiving: when chocolate which is not quite tempered is allowed to set in contact with a hard, smooth surface such as a mould, the part in contact with the mould may nevertheless set with a shiny finish. The part exposed to the air (which will be the inside surface of your moulded item), may end up looking dull and blotchy, but like the underneath of your car, does it really matter if this part is not immaculate - especially if it is going to be filled with chocolates or a centre?

Re-cooling the chocolate This is a method I discovered when the backs of my mentors were turned (I still hear them dictating to me that, if you have not tempered your chocolate successfully the first time, you must start all over again by re-heating the chocolate to the maximum recommended temperature). If you are slightly out with the tempering process, cool your chocolate until it is very thick and then reheat, whilst stirring frequently, to the recommended temperature for keeping your chocolate tempered. You might well be in for a pleasant surprise!

Polish This is not recommended! In fact, the more you rub chocolate, the more matt it becomes.

Refrigerator/freezer Bringing chocolates out from a very cold environment will induce condensation (similar to the dew that appears on the car, on a cold but sunny winter's morning) For as long as the chocolates are wet, they will appear shiny!

Lastly, remember that, even if your chocolate doesn't look perfect, it can still be enjoyed. Would you get rid of your child simply because he cannot keep his room tidy?

Excerpts from a chocolate-maker's diary

1993

September
Saturday

Chocolates inscribed 'Good to meet you', plus two roses made from chocolate, accompanied by a bottle of champagne and two glasses. Reason: a blind date (arranged through a mutual friend). Location: The Mall. Weather: cool evening, star-lit sky. Very quickly became totally smitten ... Confessed that if I was ever to reveal the highly confidential process behind my most complicated chocolate, the secret was so cherished that the next sentence would have to be to ask for her hand in marriage!

Sunday

Verdict on the chocolates (shared with a close friend and in my absence): orgasmic irresistible'. What about me? Judgement to be withheld until a later date !

October
Saturday

Chocolate soufflé. Setting: her flat. She has entrusted (!) me with her keys, so as to prepare whilst she is out for the day. Accompaniments: more champagne and candles ... Verdict: bliss!

A week later

She knows the secrets of my most cherished chocolate!

November

A minor fall-out. A box made out of chocolate with on the lid written (in chocolate) 'I'm sorry' and filled with her favourite chocolates....... I'm forgiven!

December

Layer of chocolates with the words 'Eat Me' written on them. In the next layer was the engagement ring!

1994

April

Made an egg depicting a very graceful, reclining nude with red hair ... Have never seen her consume an egg so quickly and with a face the same colour as her hair!

September

The chocolate wedding cake, festooned with peach coloured flowers (chocolate), leaves (chocolate) and ribbonned (yet again, chocolate) ... Verdict : 'Worth getting married all over again for!'

1995

January

Foetus loves chocolate - kicks more energetically when mother is eating chocolate.

March

Our son is to be named Theo after Theobroma cacao.

April

Easter Egg depicting an exasperated mother pinned between a milk-seeking baby and an attention-craving cat - egg has been kept for the family archives, along with the album.

Chapter 3

Creating your own masterpiece

If you need any additional incentive to get on with creating your own masterpiece, try reading the true-life excerpts from my diary shown opposite. I hope they will inspire you to take a leaf out of my own book - and allow chocolate to embellish your life as successfully and enjoyably as it has mine!

YOU WILL NEED

❖ **Bowl of tempered chocolate with spoon or spatula** The amount of chocolate, obviously, depends on how many chocolates you intend to make: as a rough guide, half a hollow heart might weigh 30-50 g; a solid one 80g. From a practical point of view, it is easier if the volume of chocolate in the bowl is about 1½ -2 times the total weight of your intended production.

❖ **Dry pastry or small paint brush, with soft bristles** Not essential at this stage but you will need one, or even a few, when you start marbling or painting.

❖ **Moulds** These should not pose a problem for you, the privileged owner of this kit! With scissors or craft knife, cut around the shapes if necessary. If you can, leave a small rim (about 1 cm) around the shape; later on, this will allow you to hold the mould firmly without your fingers straying inside. The mould will now need to be cleaned (see page 59).

❖ **Plastic scraper** Not essential but very handy. Can be found at most pâtisserie specialists. A palette knife or the blunt side of a knife can substitute.

❖ **Cotton wool or very soft tissue paper** Needed for cleaning or drying your moulds.

❖ **Hair dryer** Good for cleaning moulds that are not too heavily stained.

❖ **Moist (but not dripping) rag, an old tea towel and/or loads of kitchen paper towelling.**

❖ **Cooking foil** This is useful for wrapping up unused blocks of chocolate.

❖ **Comfortable posture** You may be doing a lot of bending over or stooping. A tall stool allows you to work at the right level relative to the work surface.

❖ **Good light/spotlight** Some of the work can be very intricate.

❖ **Cool, steam-free room** Ideally around 17-20°C . At this temperature, tempered chocolate normally behaves itself well but, at the same time, you are unlikely to turn hypothermic in a room this cool.

❖ **Two objects of equal height, such as blocks of wood or metal** Rest your inverted moulds on these. To keep the environmental health officer happy, cover wooden blocks in greaseproof paper. See page 31 for how these blocks are used. Placing the moulds in this elevated position will mean that, when you come to pick up the moulds and the chocolate has set firmly, they will not be stuck to your work surface.

❖ **Greaseproof paper or baking parchment** These are widely available from supermarkets. One or other is essential for making paper cones for piping and they are also useful for covering your work surface.

To make a moulded item, using just one colour or tone

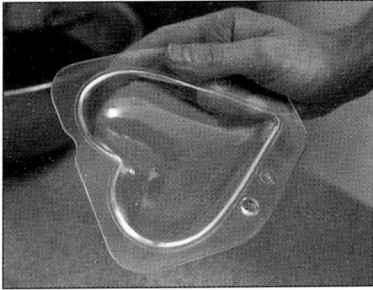

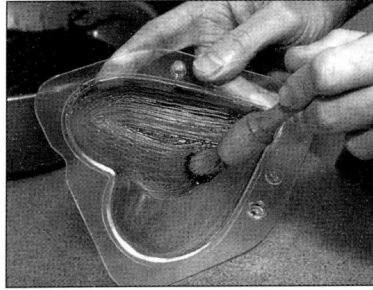

1 Take hold of your mould by the rim (if there is one). If you hold your fingers for too long over a part of the mould under which lies chocolate, the chocolate may start too soften and the final appearance of your finished product may be blemished. Moreover, resist touching the interior of the mould: fingerprints can result in chocolate sticking to the mould. Fingerprints may even transfer themselves to the finished product and be an embarrassing eyesore.

2 Stir your bowl of tempered chocolate, and apply a thin layer to the inside of the mould. I prefer to paint this on with a pastry brush, as this prevents air bubbles from lodging in the nooks and crannies of the moulds (for instance, in the points of a star), and is relatively mess-free. (An alternative is instead to simply pour chocolate directly into the mould, tip and leave to drain as for step 5(b), and proceed to step 3. Although this method is quicker, the finish is less likely to be as shiny, and the likelihood of air bubbles or pockets remaining to create a pin-pricked surface is much higher.)

3 Allow this first layer to set, by placing your mould in a cool place, ideally at 15-18°C, which can take 2-10 minutes, depending on its thickness. Using the refrigerator is fine, provided that you remove the mould before the chocolate has firmly set, after a couple of minutes or so, and let the mould return to room temperature before applying any more layers. The thinner the layer, the quicker it will set and the more likely it is that the end result will be as gleaming as a soldier's set of parade boots.

4 Repeat step 2 as soon as the chocolate is firm to the touch but has not started shrinking away from the mould. Do not worry, at this stage, if the interior is rough or uneven.

At this point, you have a choice of a solid or hollow item.

5 A *For a solid item:* This gives you a solid shape like a bar of chocolate, but thicker and, therefore, more to get your teeth into! As soon as the chocolate appears firm, fill the mould up to the rim with chocolate. Tap the mould (to remove air bubbles), level out the top (which will, in fact, become the bottom), and leave to set. If it is relatively thick (3 mm or more), it is best to accelerate the process by refrigerating the mould (bottom side up!) for a few minutes. Just as a thin film of water will

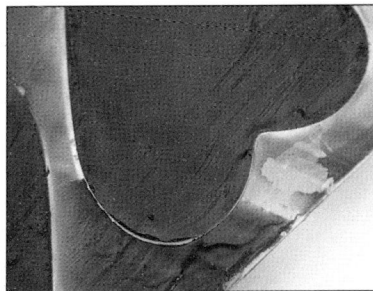

evaporate far more quickly than a deep bowl of water, a dense layer of molten chocolate will take far longer to set than a thin coating. Remember, though, that if molten chocolate is allowed too long to set, its molecular

structure will return to its naturally disorganised state (see page 18). The result would be a dull, matt or even streaky appearance. Having removed the mould from the refrigerator, put it to one side and now proceed to step 6.

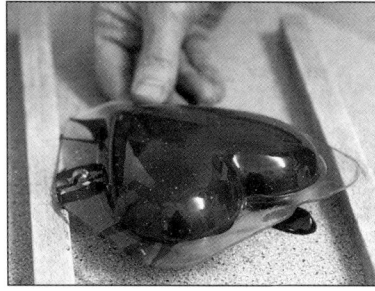

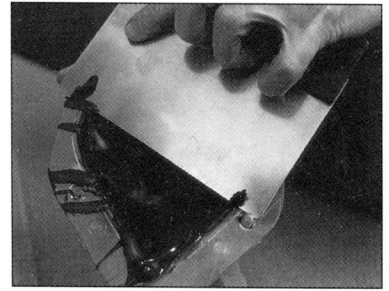

5B *For a hollow item or 'shell'*: This can be filled with a centre, or chocolates, or almost anything you wish! As soon as the chocolate is firm after step 4 spoon or pour a final layer of chocolate into the mould (this does not have to be as thin as the previous two layers) To achieve a smooth, even finish all over, tap the mould, at the same time, tilting it in different directions. Now, tip the mould upside-down over the bowl and encourage any excess chocolate to drip into the bowl, by tapping the side of the mould gently (tap too hard and your chef d'oeuvre may take a lemming-like dive into your bowl of chocolate!) Place on your blocks (still upside-down), so any further drips will land on your work surface. Leave for a couple of minutes, until the chocolate is firm but still soft enough for the next stage. Scrape clean the rim of the mould and then put to one side (if it looks as if the chocolate is taking longer than normal to set, that is, it is still visibly wet after, say, 3-4 minutes, banish the mould to the refrigerator for just a couple of minutes). Now is the moment, if you so wish, to fetch a trumpet and to triumphantly proclaim the arrival of the most exciting stage!

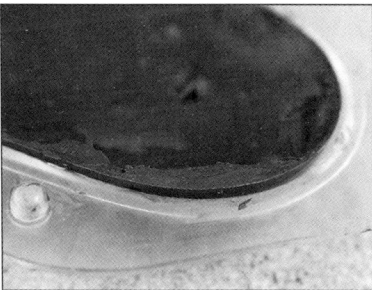

6 The finale! After a while (a few minutes to an hour or two, depending to a great extent on the temperature of the room), the chocolate will shrink away from the mould. Ideally, resist touching! It should come away completely of its own accord. But if you really are too excited to wait, you can nudge the process along by turning the mould over (in other words, plastic surface facing you) and by *gently* tapping it. The thrill experienced as your chocolate creation slips from out of its protective mould is, for me, like the wondrous moment when a baby decides to to make its entrance into the outside world. However, be warned that if you coerce your chocolate out before it is ready, you could be in for a major disappointment: it might well not come out cleanly, in which case the exterior of your composition will be irreversibly scarred.

Using two or more tones or colours to achieve a marble effect

Now is the moment when the unique world of chocolate creativity starts to open up before you, even if you do not have recourse to coloured chocolate but are confined to just plain, milk and white. The process is similar to that of making an item with just one type of chocolate, as described in the previous section. However, in the first few layers there is a difference:

I With a pastry or paint brush, stab or daub (but gently, so as not to damage the surface of the mould) small amounts of one type of tempered chocolate on to the interior of your clean mould. If you want a coloured effect, use either coloured *couverture*, or colour white chocolate (see page 13).

2 Immediately repeat the process, with another tone or colour. At this stage, you may wish to merge the two in places; the good thing about transparent moulds is that you can turn them over, and by looking through the plastic (if it is clean!) get a good idea of how the final result will appear.

3 Let this first layer set (2-5 minutes). You may wish to repeat steps 1, 2 and 3, to create greater depth and contrast, but this is optional.

4 Paint on a thin layer uniformly, as if you are painting a wall. The colour chosen will determine the general background tone of your creation. Allow to set.

5 Complete your work by following steps 5 and 6, on pages 30-31.

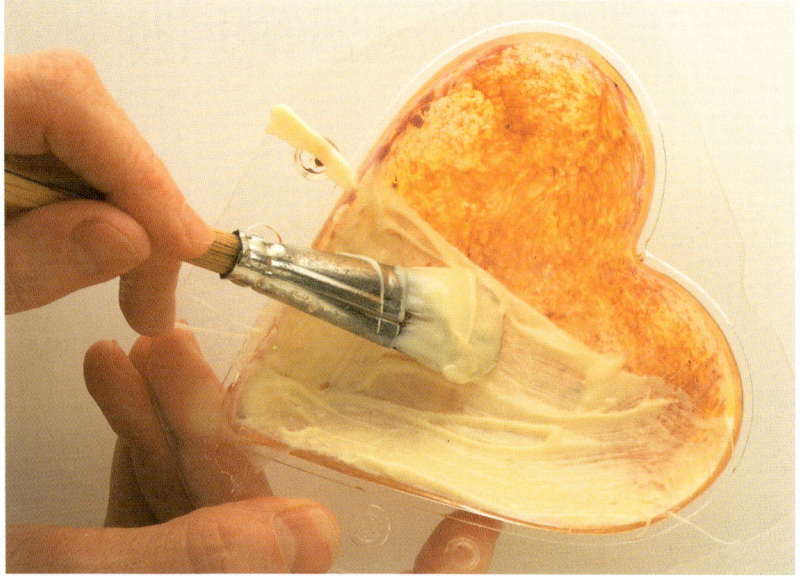

These hearts show the difference applying a final layer of white or dark background can make to the overall appearance of your masterpiece (see step 4, above).

Increasing the depth or three-dimensional appearance

This can be achieved by a simple but extremely effective use of just one colour right at the beginning, the final effect determined by your brush technique.

Stipple (as if you were applying a myriad of full stops), using just the tip of the brush; your finish may be similar to that of a thrush's egg.

Using a brush or spoon, lines of chocolate can also be dribbled on, giving a zebra-like effect (see the star on the front cover of this book, and this egg).

As always, allow this first layer to dry before going on to the next layer. However, with the exception of the stripes, this layer should be very thin and will consequently set very quickly (within a minute or two).

Make circular, whirlwind movements with your brush and a very distinctive and unusual finish can be obtained.

Stroke with the
brush in one
direction and you
can achieve a woody
appearance.

How to draw with chocolate

Extend your repertoire by mastering the art of drawing outlined shapes or letters on your masterpiece. But remember that to appear on the 'surface' of your shape this needs to be the first stage of decorating your shape.

The only additions to your stock of chocolate-making equipment are one or more very thin paintbrushes, a good supply of greaseproof paper or baking parchment, and a pair of scissors, with which to make your own piping cones. At first, these cones may appear to be a daunting origami procedure, but with a little practice I will place a small bet that you will be glad you persisted. Although it is not essential to use cones, instead relying solely on brushes, these cones will greatly increase your creative repertoire.

TECHNIQUE

Making the piping cone (the two sides of the paper have been shaded differently in order to make it clearer for you when following the photographs).

1 Cut yourself a piece of greaseproof paper, approximately 12-15 cm x 19-22 cm and cut it in half.

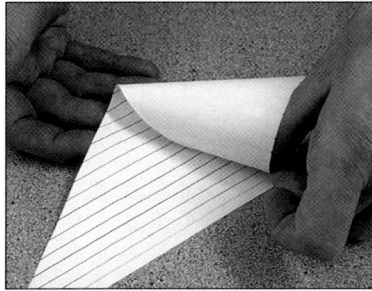

2 Fold one half as shown, to produce the beginnings of a cone. Roll the paper in such a way that the end of the funnel is as tight as possible.

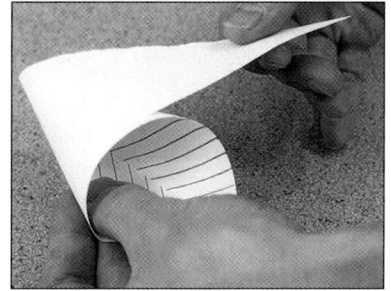

3 Wrap the remaining piece of paper around the funnel, whilst trying to keep the point as tightly closed as possible.

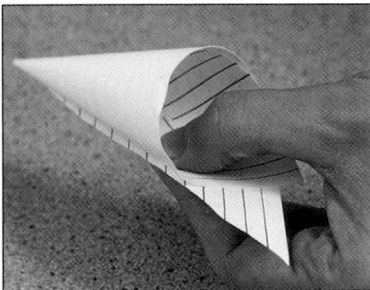

4 Tuck in the loose end.

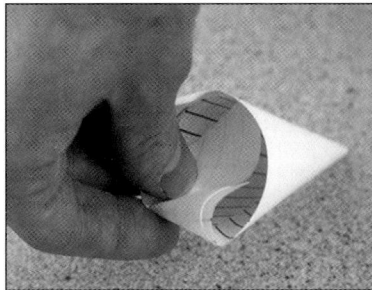

5 Fold in the longest part of the cone, so that the rim of the cone is roughly circular and the cone will not come apart when you let go.

6 Your cone should now be ready to use.

TECHNIQUE
Using the cone to draw

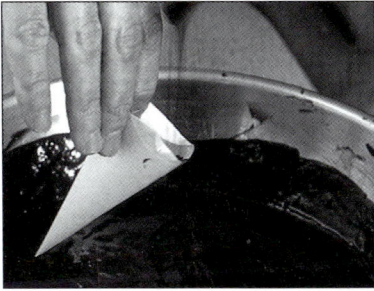

1 Spoon a small amount of lump-free, tempered chocolate into the cone, so it is no more than two-thirds full (try not to miss, since a mucky cone with chocolate dribbling down the outside can be ruinous if it drips on your masterpiece).

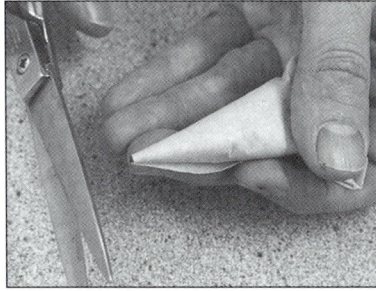

2 With a pair of scissors, cut a small hole at the point of the cone; the size of the hole determines the thickness of the line you draw. You might first want to have a practice squirt in the bowl, to ensure that the 'choco-dynamics' of your cone are as desired.

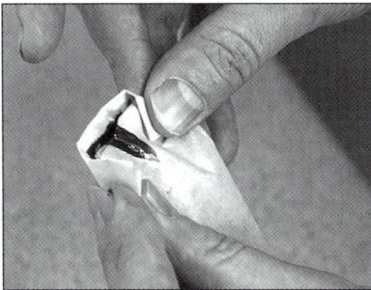

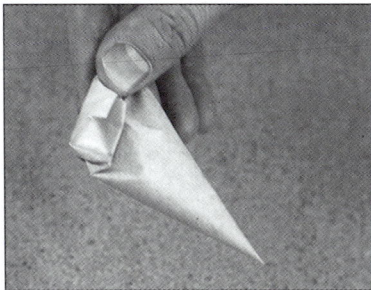

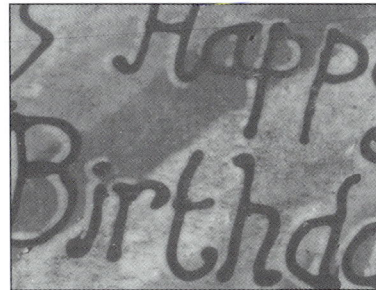

3 Seal the top of the cone, by pinching together the two opposite halves of the circle, folding the two corners over (like wrapping a parcel) and then roll it down as far as you can go (as if rolling a cigarette). This is when you discover if you have over-filled your cone, since you will then be denied the luxury of a leak-free seal!

4 You are now ready to draw simple shapes or complex outlines or even write onto the inside the mould. The lettering or shapes are the first stage, to be followed, once firm to the touch, by the other layers of chocolate, applied as previously described.

How to stick two halves of a mould together

You may want to stick two halves of the same shape - whether filled or hollow - to create a more substantial item, having first filled it with chocolates.

Glue is not recommended! Fortunately, chocolate is a very good adhesive and the following method is the easiest and cleanest. The chocolate used for piping, you may be pleased to hear, does not need to have been tempered if you are using small amounts.

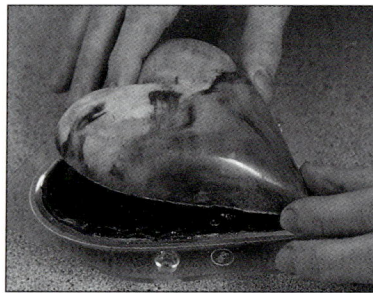

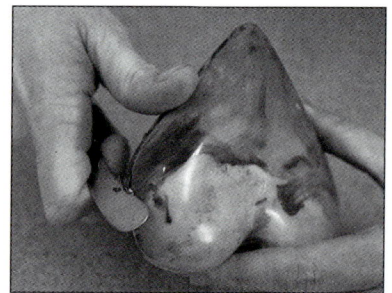

1 Replace one half in its mould. If you are enclosing chocolates, or truffles now is the moment to put them in. Make sure they are not so high as to prevent the second half from fitting tightly on top of the first. With a paper cone, carefully pipe a small amount of chocolate around the edge.

2 Before the piped chocolate sets, place the second half on top, ensuring the edges are well aligned. Leave to set (between 5 minutes and an hour, depending on how warm the chocolate used for the piping was).

3 Remove from the mould. You may need to tap the mould gently, if it is reluctant to release its occupant. Tidy the seal by carefully removing any excess chocolate glue with a knife (and cool hands!)

A sumptuous demonstration of how attractive your work of art can be when two halves are stuck together in order to present an arrangement of hand-made chocolates.

Further ideas

Impressed with your achievements so far? Well, there is even more fun to be had by exploring the almost infinite possibilities of what can be used as a mould; with your imagination now fired up, you will get more entertainment from leafing through a mould-manufacturer's catalogue than you could ever have imagined previously! However, bear in mind that the mould must be dry and preferably free of sharp corners or angles in which chocolate can get lodged. Here are some ideas to help you on your way.

❖ **Existing moulds** *(for help, please refer to the Directory)* Shop around and you may well be impressed by the range of shapes and sizes that are available. Prices can vary quite dramatically but seem to follow the general economic principle relating to supply and demand. Very specialist moulds with relatively low demand (for example, a giant Easter egg) attract painfully high prices, whereas standard sizes and shapes (for example, hearts or eggs) with high demand are very reasonably priced. The quality of the mould will also determine the price: generally the more rigid the mould, the better the quality. Moulds of relatively thin plastic are comparatively inexpensive, but the trade-offs for a low price are a shorter working life, greater tendency to being scratched or damaged and less ease of use than more rigid versions. Like your vinyl record disc, metal moulds, normally nickel-plated, are, sadly, virtually obsolete (although many are still to be found kicking around in store rooms)

having been ousted by modern-day polycarbonate, which gives good strength and durability at a substantially decreased cost.

❖ **Leaves** These are cheaper, great for decorating and more readily available than moulds! Evergreens are best, since their shiny surface give the most impressive finish and they tend to be more rigid.

1 To achieve a realistic impression and shape, use the underneath of the leaf rather than the top, and as described for decorating moulds, apply several thin layers of chocolate, to the bottom side only.

2 Once the chocolate has set, all you need do is carefully and patiently peel away the leaf from the chocolate. This is easier if your hands are cool (if not, leave your hands in the freezer for a minute or two!), and also if you have successfully avoided any run of chocolate from the bottom to the top of the leaf.

Autumn with chocolate: leaves from your garden can create very unusual and eyecatching results, as can specialist moulds like this 'woodgrained' log, or even a stationer's acetate box to make a chocolate box.

❖ **Made-to-order moulds** These tend to be phenomenally expensive (four figures!). But, in the event that you are not considering turning your humble kitchen into a commercial enterprise, you could consider making your own moulds, in which case a specialist mould supplier should be able to advise you. However, take extra care that the materials used are safe in conjunction with food.

❖ **Boxes** This is when adaptability becomes the name of the game. If you can find an empty acetate or plastic box lid kicking around, try coating the inside of it. Use lots of layers of chocolate for strength, and follow the basic mouldwork steps shown on pages 32-33.

❖ **Circular discs** Did you ever imagine that those bits of round, transparent plastic that come with your cartons of supermarket cream can be turned into chocolate coasters or Frisbees? The steps are the same as for using any of the other moulds described.

❖ **Spoons** Coat the inside of a spoon, but not the handle, and you can make impressive, small plaques or even badges! Again, use the same steps as you would when using a larger mould, although you will of course want to use far smaller quantities of chocolate. The results can make very attractive personalized cake decorations.

Chocolate Pop Art. These are a few examples of what can be done using such diverse and impromptu moulds as acetate boxes, plastic lids and the inside of a spoon. For well-defined lines, you will want to use the piping techniques described on pages 36-37, before building up any coloured background.

Chapter 4

Suitable partners for hand of chocolate in marriage

Imagine, I am the host at a dinner party and I need some new ideas for my chocolates. I suggest it is time to hand them out and nobody disagrees. Like a magician, I discreetly steer somebody towards a specific chocolate. 'Try this one,' I say. 'What is it?' 'I'll tell you after you've tasted it.' 'Mmmmm, that's really nice! Now tell me what it is.' 'Tomato.' Shock horror 'Never! Well, I am surprised. It really works. I wonder what else you can mix with chocolate?' Into action springs my mental pen and notebook!

The range of potential partners with which chocolate can be successfully married is, as I am still enjoyably discovering, awesome. Long ago, I ceased classifying chocolate as a member of the sugar family and now I think of it as an essential ingredient in its own right, which could stand its ground with many kinds of spices, fruits or vegetables. I have found it enjoying harmonious relationships with rhubarb or gooseberry, with dill, or garden mint. I have added it to vinegar or mustard. I have spiced it up with caraway seeds or paprika. I have blended it with basil or marjoram. And the result? 'The best chocolates I have ever tasted' was an oft-repeated tune, irrespective of a person's nationality, gender or age.

I hope, by sharing some of my discoveries with you, that the following recipes will prove to be a fascinating and enjoyable insight into exploring perhaps hitherto unknown sides of the personality of chocolate, although I will not ignore some of the more familiar and popular companions to chocolate, such as praline. All ingredients are widely available, equipment is nothing out of the ordinary and the methods described do not require you to be a catering wizard!

These recipes are for those who choose to be calorifically-innumerate, for they are based on the French format known as *ganache* (for which there is, woefully, no suitable English translation, though I could suggest 'Blow any idea of going on a diet!'), which describes my style of centres. 'Ganache' implies a high proportion of chocolate (hence, every recipe will be a shade of brown), lavishly mixed with copious amounts of cream and with some butter thrown in for good measure. If you are looking for ways to assuage your guilt, I recommend: 'You only live once!' or 'What the hell!' or 'A little won't do you any harm' or even 'Tomorrow, I'll run a marathon.'

There are several options for how to apply these ganache recipes, which are described at the end of this chapter.

Without any more ado, I shall now indulge in a neologism and, using an expression I coined that seems to roll teasingly off the tongue, wish you a *'bon ganaching'*!

NOTES
On making ganaches

❖ If you are making a large batch of chocolates, avoid the laborious and blister-productive task of chopping chocolate. Instead, melt the chocolate, let it cool to around 40°C and add it to the boiled cream only when the cream has cooled to 40°C or less. If either is too hot, your chocolate may separate, leaving an unsightly layer of grease floating on top.

❖ Before adding alcohol to a mixture of cream and chocolate, it is important that you allow the mixture to cool to 40°C or less. If not, the chocolate may separate.

❖ If the chocolate separates, reverse this by letting the mixture set until it is almost solid and then reheat very gently, stirring frequently, until the mixture is smooth and homogenous.

❖ The best method for softening butter is to heat it in the microwave for, say, 30 seconds at a time on medium power. Otherwise, place the bowl containing the butter over a saucepan, half-filled with hot water.

❖ When alcohol, such as rum or port, is included in a recipe, it is not necessary to use your finest bottle, since some of the subtle nuances and tones of flavours of more expensive versions might be lost when combined with chocolate.

❖ If the chocolate does not melt entirely after you have added the cream and allowed it to cool, heat the bowl very gently, stirring frequently, until it does.

YOU WILL NEED
For the ganache recipes

❖ **Thick-based saucepans** You need one or more and the thicker the bottom, the lower is the risk of burning your ingredients, which could adversely affect the flavour.

❖ **Spoon, spatula or balloon whisk** For stirring.

❖ **Mixing bowls** A variety of sizes is useful.

❖ **Bain-marie or microwave** This is useful, but not essential, for melting the chocolate and butter.

❖ **Weighing scales** These do not need to be hyper-sensitive; the recipes can tolerate slight changes without the taste being significantly affected.

❖ **Chopping board and large, sharp knife** Preferably one you don't use for onions and garlic.

❖ **Sieve or strainer** For straining out some flavourings.

❖ **Food processor or liquidizer** For finely chopping and for blending (it's only absolutely necessary in one recipe).

Use a sharp, large knife to chop chocolate. The most efficient method is to hold the handle with one hand and place the palm of your hand at the other end of the knife (using the blunt end, of course!) – see picture at left. By applying equal force to both hands and using a rocking motion, you can cut up large chunks.

Christmas pudding

Makes about 100 chocolates or fills about 30 hearts

The mention of Christmas pudding, wonderful invention that it is, nevertheless causes my stomach to moan in protest at the thought that, once a year, it will be called upon to perform a task beyond the call of duty. To top a main course of a size and variety that would normally defy imagination with one of the most filling puddings ever conceived, seems to me pure masochism. So, at the end of the meal, what better way is there to enjoy the taste of Christmas pudding than in the guise of comfortably and sensibly proportioned chocolates? My version can also be respectably enjoyed at any time of the year, if you change the name from 'Christmas pudding' to 'rum and raisin'!

The orange segments, raisins and cherries in the recipe give the ganache a rough texture, so it lends itself to being used as a filling (complementing perfectly a chocolate star, if you wish to be festive) rather than as a truffle. As for which chocolate to coat the ganache in, my personal preference is for dark: the plain chocolate counter-balances the sweetness of the centre.

YOU WILL NEED

30 ML (*2 tablespoons*) STRONGLY BREWED ASSAM TEA, STRAINED
230 G PLAIN CHOCOLATE OF ABOUT 60% COCOA SOLIDS, CHOPPED
50 G (*4 tablespoons*) RAISINS
30 G (*6 pieces*) GLACÉ CHERRIES
130 ML (*8½ tablespoons*) DOUBLE CREAM
50 G (*2 tablespoons*) MARMALADE, THE MORE BITTER, THE BETTER
50 G (*2 tablespoons*) PURE MAPLE SYRUP
6 PINCHES OF GROUND NUTMEG
4 PINCHES OF GROUND CINNAMON
¼ TEASPOON YEAST EXTRACT, E.G. MARMITE
125 G (*10 tablespoons*) UNSALTED BUTTER, SOFTENED
15 ML (*1 tablespoon*) RUM

TECHNIQUE

1 Brew the tea.
2 Put the chopped chocolate in a bowl, large enough to take all the other ingredients later on.
3 Put the raisins and cherries in a food processor and chop them finely. This can also be done by hand, giving a coarser texture, more reminiscent of a Christmas pudding since food processors tend to chop very finely.
4 Put raisins and cherries into a small saucepan and add tea. Bring to the boil and simmer gently for a few minutes, until the raisins and cherries have soaked up most of the liquid.
5 Meanwhile, measure the cream into a medium-size saucepan and add the marmalade, maple syrup, nutmeg, cinnamon and yeast extract. Bring to the boil, stirring every minute or so.
6 Put the butter to soften; it should be runny but still opaque.
7 Once the cream is boiling, add the raisins, cherries and tea, boil and stir gently for another minute, then take off the heat for a minute or so.
8 Add the hot cream to the chopped chocolate and stir until all the chocolate has melted.
9 Leave the cream and chocolate aside to cool to around body temperature (about 35°C) then add the softened butter and rum. Your ganache is ready for the next stage (see pages 54-56).

GERARD'S TIPS

Other types of tea, such as lapsang souchong or jasmine, can be used to add further subtle flavours to your ganache.

I enjoy experimenting with different types of honey and syrups, rather than just using sugar to sweeten, as they can bring additional, interesting and distinctive flavours to recipes.

You may think that yeast extract must be a printing error but, in fact, a little skillfully combats what might otherwise be a cloyingly sweet recipe!

Orange segments in the marmalade will soften during boiling and should break into smaller pieces when stirred.

As-bitter-as-you-want-it truffle

Makes about 80 chocolates or fills about 18 hearts

Whilst I relish the challenge of finding compatible mates for chocolate, in the following recipe chocolate is given an opportunity to take the stage alone. The volume of the performance is under your control, through selecting the bitterness of the chocolate you use. I have given it full voice here, by choosing chocolate of 100 per cent cocoa solids. The truffle made from this ganache will stand firm against the strongest of after-dinner espressos but, if you want a less bitter or acidic finish, simply replace some or all of the 100 per cent chocolate with a less bitter version.

This ganache is suitable for filling already-made chocolate shells and for hand-rolled chocolates. My preference for what chocolate to use for coating is for plain, rather than milk or white. Alternatively, make a distinctive drinking chocolate: simply add four or five teaspoons of ganache to a mug of boiling milk.

YOU WILL NEED

170 ML (*11 tablespoons*) SINGLE CREAM
⅓ VANILLA POD
50 G PLAIN CHOCOLATE OF 100% COCOA SOLIDS, FINELY CHOPPED
185 G PLAIN CHOCOLATE OF 55-60% COCOA SOLIDS, FINELY CHOPPED
1 LARGE EGG YOLK
40 G (*3 tablespoons +1 teaspoon*) UNSALTED BUTTER

TECHNIQUE

1 Measure the cream into a saucepan, add the vanilla pod and gently bring to the boil. Put the chocolate in a bowl that is large enough to take all the other ingredients.
2 Take the boiling cream off the heat, remove the vanilla pod and add the egg yolk stirring continuously.
3 Immediately pour the contents of the saucepan on to the chopped chocolate, stir until all the chocolate has melted, and put to one side.
4 Soften the butter, until runny but not transparent.
5 Once the mixture of cream and chocolate is tepid to the touch (about 40°C), add the softened butter. Your ganache is now ready for the next stage (see pages 54-56).

GERARD'S TIPS

See the Directory (page 61-62), for help in finding sources of chocolate of 100 per cent cocoa solids.

You may, rightly, have noticed that the combination of cream, egg yolk and vanilla in step 2 is reminiscent of a vanilla custard. This gives the ganache a more rounded finish. Vanilla is, in itself, no stranger to chocolate, since it is found in most chocolate bars.

Lemon and tarragon ganache

Makes about 60 chocolates or fills about 14 hearts

The world of chocolate is not immune to prejudice: I have come across those who adamantly believe that dark chocolate is superior to any other colour; some extremists will judge your palate to be of an inferior quality if you admit a liking for milk or white chocolate. Well, there is no redder a rag to my choleric bull than to judge people according to their preference for chocolate and, in my rage, on one occasion I dared to challenge a group of French tasters, amongst whose ranks I knew existed those guilty of chocolate *'snobisme'*. I presented for judgement a lemon ganache coated in milk chocolate. *Quelle horreur!* My attempt at conversion failed miserably but, fortunately, I had plucked up enough diplomacy and self-control to present other chocolates, which had been staidly finished in dark chocolate. My *faux pas* was soon forgotten as they swooned over these perfect specimens

and my departure saw me with a prestigious diploma as well as the realisation that I cannot change the world. Upon returning to England, it was hard not to swell up with patriotism when highly respected experts based in this country affirmed my conviction that my lemon ganache is much better covered in milk chocolate than in dark. Why not experiment yourself: wherever your loyalties lie, it will be an interesting exercise as to how the character of a ganache can be radically affected by the choice of chocolate used for the coating.

This ganache is equally suitable for filling already-made chocolate shells or for turning into chocolates.

My personal preference is to finish this ganache with milk chocolate, which removes the acidity from the ganache and, overall, gives it a more rounded character.

YOU WILL NEED

½ MEDIUM-SIZE LEMON *(about 80 g)*
100 ML *(just under 7 tablespoons)* DOUBLE CREAM
15 G *(½ tablespoon)* THIN-CUT LEMON SHRED MARMALADE
½ TEASPOON SUGAR
¼ TEASPOON FREEZE-DRIED TARRAGON
140 G PLAIN CHOCOLATE OF 55-65% MINIMUM COCOA SOLIDS, FINELY CHOPPED
25 G MILK CHOCOLATE
30 G *(2 generous tablespoons)* UNSALTED BUTTER

GERARD'S TIP

The tarragon isn't essential but it does add extra character to the ganache

---

TECHNIQUE

1 Wash and dry the half-lemon and further cut it in three to four pieces, leaving the rind on.

2 Measure the cream into a saucepan and add the pieces of lemon, the marmalade, sugar and tarragon.

3 Gently bring the cream to the boil and then leave to simmer for 3-5 minutes, for the lemon to soften.

4 Place the chopped chocolate in a bowl large enough for all the ingredients.

5 Remove the cream from the heat and pour into a strainer held over the bowl of chocolate. With a spoon or spatula, encourage all the cream and juices from the lemon to pass through the strainer. Stir the chocolate and cream until the chocolate has melted and put to one side.

6 Soften the butter, until runny but not transparent.

7 Once the mixture of cream and chocolate is tepid to the touch (about 40°C), add the softened butter. Your ganache is now ready for the next stage (see pages 54-56).

Chestnut ganache

Makes about 180 chocolates or fills about 45 hearts

'Some say sex is better than chocolate. But I think chocolate is better than sex.' These are not my words but those of a committed devotée of chocolate when asked on camera how she rated this food. You may not necessarily agree with her but, nevertheless, for chocolate even to be compared to man's supposed most pleasurable and God-given gift is testimony itself. As to where chocolate comes in my own league-table of greatest sources of pleasure, it would be indiscreet to reveal here where my loyalties lie: instead, I elect to err on the side of diplomacy and suggest you try these two celestial pursuits together! The ganache that can send me into the dizziest heights of rapturous bliss is made from chestnuts, although to appreciate its heavenliness to the full, it does help if you are a fan of chestnuts in the first place.

There is, however, one potential flaw in this ganache: it has a very short shelf-life of around one week. But then, as somebody I recall said: 'What do you mean this is a problem? It's a legitimate excuse to pig out!'

Since the proportion of chocolate to cream and other ingredients is lower than normal, when set, this ganache is relatively very soft and friable. It is, therefore, more suited to be a filling for already-made chocolate shells than to be turned into a hand-rolled truffle. If there is any left, why not save it and use it as a filling for a cake?

YOU WILL NEED

440 G UNSWEETENED CHESTNUT PURÉE
220 ML DOUBLE CREAM
35 G *(7 teaspoons)* WHITE SUGAR
150 G PLAIN CHOCOLATE OF LESS THAN 65% COCOA SOLIDS
150 G MILK CHOCOLATE
75 G *(about 5½ tablespoons)* UNSALTED BUTTER
45 ML *(3 tablespoons)* RUM

GERARD'S TIPS

Chestnut purée normally comes in 440 g cans. A whole can makes a large quantity of ganache but it freezes well.

Use either caster or granulated sugar, because the size of grains of sugar doesn't matter as the sugar completely dissolves.

I wouldn't use a bitter chocolate, of more than 65 per cent cocoa solids, because its acidic taste would be detrimental to the overall flavour and balance of the ganache.

My addition of milk chocolate gives a rounded, milky texture.

TECHNIQUE

1 Put the chestnut purée, double cream and sugar in a saucepan and heat gently, until the mixture is boiling. It is important to stir frequently, preventing the chestnut in contact with the bottom of the pan from burning, as well as commencing the process of breaking up the purée and mixing it in with the cream.
2 Once the mixture has started to boil, transfer to the liquidizer or food processor and blend until the mixture is smooth and homogeneous. Leave to one side to cool until tepid, which will take an hour or two.
3 Melt the chocolate in the microwave or a bain-marie (see pages 22-23).
4 Soften the butter until it is runny but still opaque.
5 When the mixture of cream and chestnut is tepid (around 40°C), add the melted chocolate and mix thoroughly.
6 Mix in the softened butter and the rum. Your ganache is now ready for the next stage (see pages 54-56).

Port and clove ganache

Makes about 80 whisked truffles or fills about 16 hearts

Despite many attempts, with and without the coercion of others, I have never managed to fall in love with beer. Consequently, the attraction of pubs is lost on me and, instead, I pine for the return of England in the seventeenth and eighteenth centuries, when chocolate-drinking-houses threatened to become more popular than ale-houses. How I yearn for the appeal of chocolate to be so strong that, like beer, it becomes the focal point for social gatherings of great merriment or for earnest debate. Wouldn't it be wonderful, so I dream, if variations of your chocolate brew were again readily on tap, with the addition of rum, whisky, or any alcohol or concoction of spices. As I dream, whilst researching the chocolate archives, I came across one of the first-ever recipes relating to the chocolate-drinking-house era. It suggested port be added to the chocolate. Here was history confirming my own discovery that port makes a good partner for chocolate. In my recipe below, albeit for eating and not drinking, I hope you will agree with history and me that, when port and chocolate are delicately balanced, the result is extremely gratifying. If you need any further justification for launching into this recipe, how about taking solace from the medical research that, in 1996, confirmed that the combination of red wine and chocolate can reduce the long-term risk of heart disease?

I strongly recommend turning this ganache into a whisked truffle (see page 56), coating it in milk chocolate and rolling it in cocoa powder. The ganache itself, is very rich and is made lighter by beating air into it. Its intensity and sharpness is counterbalanced by the milk chocolate. Any lingering sweetness from the milk chocolate is then removed by the bitterness of the cocoa powder.

This is not to say that this recipe is not suitable simply for using as a filling just as it is. In fact, one of the favourite pastimes of our toddler son is to stick a spoon into a bowl of this ganache and consume as if it was ice cream!

Moreover, returning to the historical theme, try melting five or so cocoa-dusted port truffles in a mug of boiling milk and enjoy as a nightcap.

YOU WILL NEED

100 ML *(just under 7 tablespoons)* DOUBLE CREAM
4 PINCHES OF GROUND CLOVES
220 G PLAIN CHOCOLATE OF MINIMUM 55-60% COCOA SOLIDS, FINELY CHOPPED
50 G *(just under 2 tablespoons)* UNSALTED BUTTER
60 ML *(4 tablespoons)* PORT

GERARD'S TIP

The overall flavour of the ganache will be affected by the type of port you use but it isn't necessary to use your oldest and most expensive bottle. A supermarket ruby or tawny version will give a very satisfactory result.

TECHNIQUE

1 Measure the cream into a saucepan, add the cloves and bring to the boil. Put the chocolate in a bowl big enough to hold all the other ingredients.
2 Once the cream has started to boil, pour it over the chocolate and stir until the chocolate has melted. Put to one side.
3 Soften the butter, until runny but not transparent.
4 Once the mixture of cream and chocolate is tepid to the touch (around 40°C), add the softened butter and port. Your ganache is now ready for the next stage (see page 56).

An illusion of praline

Makes about 60 chocolates or fills about 15 hearts

'Boring old praline' were the words of a particular journalist who had obviously had more than her fair share. I admit that this version of nuts has been done to death, not just by the Belgians but also, surprisingly, by the French. Nevertheless, in small amounts, I remain a supporter of praline. To make it at home, however, is not a particularly enticing prospect, since it can be a hot, steamy, long and delicate process. The nuts (normally almonds, but could be other nuts, or even a mixture such as almonds and hazelnuts) have to be caramelized and then crushed to a very fine, smooth paste. To buy your own praline is an equally taxing ordeal, since it is, infuriatingly, not generally available for sale to the public in small amounts. However, Robert-the-Bruce-style, averse to admitting defeat, I have concocted the following worthy and easily accessible imitation of a praline ganache.

This ganache is equally suitable for filling chocolate shells or for turning into chocolates.

I prefer to finish this ganache with plain chocolate, to counteract the sweetness of the amaretto and the hazelnut spread.

YOU WILL NEED

120 ML *(8 tablespoons)* DOUBLE CREAM
60 G *(3 tablespoons)* CHOCOLATE HAZELNUT SPREAD
25 G *(3 tablespoons)* GROUND ALMONDS
110 G PLAIN CHOCOLATE, FINELY CHOPPED
20 G *(about 1½ tablespoons)* UNSALTED BUTTER
20 ML *(4 teaspoons)* AMARETTO LIQUEUR

TECHNIQUE

1 Measure the cream, hazelnut spread and ground almonds into a pan and gently bring to the boil. Put the chocolate in a bowl big enough to hold all the other ingredients.
2 Once the cream has started to boil, pour it over the chocolate and stir until the chocolate has melted. Put to one side.
3 Soften the butter, until runny but not transparent.
4 Once the mixture of cream and chocolate has cooled to around body temperature (about 35°C), add the softened butter and amaretto liqueur. Your ganache is now ready for the next stage (see pages 54-56).

GERARD'S TIPS

The pre-ground almonds sold in supermarkets are of a particle size that gives an interesting texture, reminiscent of coconut.

The chocolate solids in chocolate hazelnut spread are relativly low and so I would recommend using a more bitter chocolate to compensate, above 60% cocoa solids.

Rose and fennel

Makes about 50 chocolates or fills around 14 hearts

Chocolate, as you undoubtedly already know, is often accused of being an aphrodisiac, thanks to an enzyme known as phenylethylamine. In fact, Aztec women were forbidden from drinking chocolate, lest the menfolk lost their women as they wandered astray in an aphrodisiac trance! How much more romantic can you get than to combine chocolate with the modern-day symbol of love (namely, a heart), a bunch of red roses (painted on to the heart by your own fair hands) and a centre oozing with the taste of roses!

But you do not have to be feeling romantic to enjoy this centre. The addition of fennel and ginger make it an interesting and pleasurable culinary foray in its own right.

This ganache is equally suitable for filling already-made chocolate shells or for turning into chocolates.

A dark, milk or white chocolate coating works equally well with this ganache, although the actual character of the ganache will change with the choice of coating.

YOU WILL NEED

100 ML *(6 tablespoons + 2 teaspoons)* DOUBLE CREAM
4 ML *(⁴⁄₅ teaspoon)* CONCENTRATED ROSE-WATER
2 PINCHES OF GROUND GINGER
¼ TEASPOON FENNEL SEED
115 G PLAIN CHOCOLATE OF 55-65% COCOA SOLIDS
50 G MILK CHOCOLATE
40 G UNSALTED BUTTER

TECHNIQUE

1 Measure the cream into a saucepan and add the rose-water, ginger and fennel to the saucepan.
2 Slowly bring the cream to the boil, stirring regularly every minute or so. Put the plain and milk chocolate in a bowl that will be large enough to take the other ingredients later on.
3 Take the cream off the boil and, without too much delay, pour this cream through a sieve or strainer on to the chocolate.
4 Stir the chocolate and cream, until the the the chocolate has melted. Now, put this mixture to one side.
5 Soften the butter until it is runny, but still opaque.
6 When the combined mixture of cream and chocolate has cooled to around body temperature (about 35°C), add the butter and mix gently. Your ganache is ready for the next stage (see pages 54-56).

GERARD'S TIPS

Concentrated rose-water is available from most chemists.

The milk chocolate is added to give a more rounded, creamier taste to the overall flavour.

Rose-water needs to be boosted with other flavours. The basic harmonies of a symphony can be played on just one instrument but an orchestra adds greatly to the character and strength of the piece; similarly, in the case of this recipe, ginger and fennel are the supporting instruments but you might like to experimiment with alternative spices, such as cinnamon, nutmeg or even ground bay leaf.

What to do with your ganache

*Now that you have finished your ganache but it is still warm enough to be runny,
your next actions will be determined by the fate you have in mind for it.*

TO FILL A PREVIOUSLY MADE, HOLLOW SHELL (SEE PAGE 30-31).
This could be an egg, star or heart, or any other moulded shape such as a Belgian-style chocolate.

TECHNIQUE

YOU WILL NEED
HOLLOW SHELL
GANACHE
TEMPERED CHOCOLATE
TEASPOON, OR
PIPING BAG WITH
10-13 MM NOZZLE OR
PROFESSIONAL DISPENSER
SCRAPER, PALETTE KNIFE OR KNIFE

1 As soon as you have finished preparing your ganache and whilst it is still runny, fill the chocolate shell (you might find this easier if the shell is in its mould) to within 1-3 mm of its rim. Use a teaspoon, piping bag or dispenser.

2 Gently tap or rock the shell or mould, so that the ganache is evenly distributed.

3 Put the ganache-filled shell aside, to allow the ganache to set firmly before the next stage, for which you will need some tempered chocolate. At room temperature, it may take from an hour to several hours before the ganache is firm enough. Alternatively, the process can be accelerated, by placing the ganache-filled shell in the refrigerator for anything between a quarter to one hour, but it must be allowed to reach room temperature (about 15-30 minutes) before going on to the next stage.

4 To cap the ganache-filled shell, spoon on a thin layer of tempered chocolate and, before the chocolate has time to set, quickly spread it evenly over the mould using a scraper, palette knife or the straight edge of a knife. Practice makes perfect: my first-ever attempt at this saw more chocolate on my hands and clothes than on the mould and the finish looked as if somebody had taken a scouring brush to the chocolate.

5 Allow the cap to set firmly, so that it can be seen to be shrinking away from the mould. This may take anywhere between 15 minutes to a couple of hours, and may need to be helped along by a short stretch (around 10 minutes) in the refrigerator. Whilst keeping the mould close to your work surface, carefully turn it over. Your finished shell should just slip out of its mould, albeit with a gentle tap or two against the side.

To convert your ganache into a hand-rolled truffle
This is recommended especially for the As-bitter-as-you-want-it truffle (see page 48).

Technique

You will need
Ganache
Teaspoon, or
Piping bag with 10-13mm nozzle
Kitchen paper towelling
Greaseproof paper,
baking parchment or cooking foil
Damp cloth
Tempered chocolate

1 Allow your ganache to set to a semi-solid state, stirring every quarter of an hour or so, until it is soft enough to be coerced into the shape you desire and yet firm enough to remain in that shape. It may take anything from a quarter of an hour to several hours before your ganache is ready, depending on the amount made and on the temperature where it has been left.

2A When the ganache is ready, make roughly shaped balls of about 2-3 cm diameter by using a piping bag.

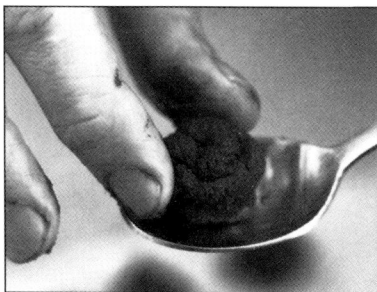

2B Alternatively, scoop with a teaspoon and shape with your fingers, wiping the spoon clean with some kitchen paper towelling after each chocolate. In both cases, leave the ganache to set on either greaseproof paper or cooking foil. The time taken depends on the temperature at which you leave it; about an hour if in the refrigerator and about 3-5 hours if the room temperature is around 18-20°C.

3 Once firm, you can improve the roundness, if you so wish, by rolling the piece of ganache in the palm of your hand. (You will need a cloth to hand, in order to remove the build-up of chocolate on the palm of your hand from time to time, which will, otherwise, make it increasingly difficult to roll.)

4 When the truffle balls are firm, from a bowl of tempered chocolate, scoop up a small amount of chocolate, using the tips of your ring, middle and index fingers, and deposit it on the palm of the opposite hand. With thumb and index finger, pick up a ball of ganache, place it in the palm which contains the pool of chocolate and roll the ball around until it is totally covered in chocolate, as evenly as possible.

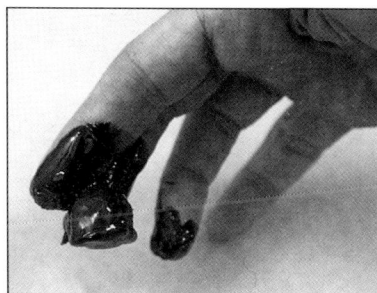

5 Scoop up the coated truffle and carefully place it on a clean sheet of greaseproof paper or foil. Leave to set, which, if the chocolate is well tempered and the room temperature is cool (under 20°C), should only take a matter of minutes. Leave for at least a further hour or so, if you want the coating to be crisp and crunchy.

To convert your ganache into a cocoa-dusted truffle

This is ideal if your chocolate for coating is not perfectly tempered. or for providing extra flavouring or a foil to a very sweet centre.

Technique

You will need
Ganache
Spoon or piping bag with
10-13 mm nozzle
Kitchen paper towelling
Greaseproof paper,
baking parchment or cooking foil
Damp cloth
Tempered chocolate
Cocoa powder
Fork
Sieve or strainer

1 Proceed as for How to convert your ganache into a hand-rolled truffle, steps 1-5 (see page 55). However, the coating in step 5 should, ideally, be very thin, since another coat is going to be applied in the next stage.

2 Repeat step 5, coating your truffle with a second thin layer of chocolate. This time, however, do not leave to set but instead drop the wet truffle into a tray or bowl of cocoa powder. Do this carefully, otherwise you will forever be cleaning your room of cocoa powder! With the back of a fork gently move it around until it is completely coated in cocoa powder (the fork will leave an attractive ridged effect at the same time). Leave to set for at least 10 minutes.

3 Remove the truffles from the cocoa powder (this can be done with your hands; the sensation of good-quality cocoa powder passing through your fingers is like touching warm velvet!). You will need a damp cloth nearby for your hands. Place the truffles in a sieve or strainer. Hold the strainer over the cocoa powder and gently tap it, to remove any excess powder.

To convert your ganache into a whisked truffle

This gives a lighter, mousse-like texture, and is especially recommended for the port ganache, using milk chocolate, and rolling the truffles in cocoa powder as above.

Technique

You will need
Ganache
Electric whisk
Spoon or piping bag with
10-13 mm nozzle
Kitchen Towelling
Greaseproof paper,
baking parchment or cooking foil
Damp cloth
Tempered chocolate
Cocoa powder
Fork
Sieve or Strainer

1 Before proceeding as for 'How to convert your ganache into a hand-rolled truffle', steps 1-4 (see page 55), whilst the ganache in the bowl is starting to firm up, intermittently whisk it. (Whisking when the ganache is still warm and relatively runny will not achieve anything.) As when you whisk egg whites, the ganache will increase in volume (it may almost double); unlike egg whites, the colour will get significantly lighter. Whilst whisking, you may need to scrape off ganache that has set on the side of the bowl and move it into the path of the

> ### Gerard's Tip
>
> *To convert your ganache into a stick shape like the ones on page 39, instead of using a teaspoon or piping bag and nozzle to achieve a round shape, pipe the ganache in long, straight lines on to greaseproof paper or baking parchment. When set, cut into shorter lengths and finish as you desire, by coating in just chocolate or in a combination of chocolate and cocoa powder.*

paddles, thereby ensuring your ganache is of a consistent texture and free of lumps. Now proceed, before the ganache sets firmly.

Chapter 5

The haberdashery of chocolate

Mastering chocolate-making is like learning how to drive around London! The going can be less frustrating, more rewarding and shorter once you come across the short cuts. To help you through the maze and to minimize the risk of road rage (or rather chocolate rage), here are my own tips.

HOW TO STORE BLOCKS OF CHOCOLATE/*COUVERTURE*

The French words of warning found on some makes of *couverture* colourfully sum up the ideal conditions: *'Craint la chaleur et l'humidité'* (is scared of heat and humidity). More precisely, the optimum temperature for storing chocolate is 15-18°C. Normally, however, your coolest room should suffice, especially if you go through your chocolate quickly. If you keep it in the refrigerator, dry any condensation that may form on the surface with kitchen paper towelling, after taking it out of the refrigerator and before using the chocolate.

❖ The relative humidity should be less than 60 per cent. In other words, it is best to store your chocolate away from damp or steamy conditions, such as might be found in the kitchen or in the basement.

❖ Chocolate should be kept away from light: keep in its original packaging or wrap it up in foil.

❖ Chocolate should be kept away from strong smells, such as fresh paint or fish, since it can absorb them (unless of course you like fish-flavoured chocolate!). This is particularly relevant for molten chocolate.

HOW TO STORE CHOCOLATES THAT CONTAIN CREAM AND BUTTER

The cooler the temperature at which the chocolates are stored, the longer they will stay fresh. As a rough guide, the ganaches mentioned in this book will, if coated immediately (the chocolate coating protects the centre, to some extent), last around two weeks if kept at 21°C, at least three weeks at 18°C and four or more weeks if kept refrigerated. The exception is chestnut ganache, which should be eaten within a week.

If chocolates are kept in the refrigerator, and you want to keep them looking pristine, beware of sugar blooming. Like dew forming on your car on a sunny, crisp autumn morning, condensation forms on cold chocolate if it is exposed to a relatively warmer environment. This moisture causes the sugar molecules in the chocolate to dissolve. Therefore, as the condensation dries, the surface of your chocolates will change from being wet and glistening to being sticky and dusty/mottled in appearance, and may finally end up feeling rough to the touch and looking stale. The taste however is not affected. The risk of sugar bloom can be reduced by delaying opening your box of chocolates for around 15 minutes after removing it from the refrigerator.

❖ Chocolates, surprisingly, can be frozen but, to avoid sugar bloom, a combination of a large amount of insulation around the chocolates with a patient and gradual step-by-step transfer from freezer to refrigerator to room over many hours will be needed.

HOW TO STORE YOUR MOULDED WORKS OF ART

Over time, the brilliant sheen exhibited by chocolate that has just left its mould will, sadly, fade: the difference between a new-born chocolate and one a couple of days old is noticeable to the trained eye of a perfectionist. Happily, there are ways of slowing down this ageing process, if you so wish.

❖ Keep your finished product away from warm

temperatures (ideally it should be stored at around 15-18°C). Fat bloom, (alternatively known as 'cocoa butter bloom') is another scourge of chocolate, which also causes it to lose its sheen and to take on a whitish, stale appearance. Heat allows the microscopic cocoa butter molecules (which the tempering process had organised into a uniform structure), to revert to a random structure of different sizes and forms. Fat bloom can be told from sugar bloom in that, with the former, the surface remains smooth to the touch, it may not break with a clear resounding snap, and its taste might be affected (caused by the different cocoa-butter molecules melting in the mouth at different rates).

❖ Try not to expose chocolate to cold temperatures, such as those of a refrigerator (sugar bloom, discussed above, will mercilessly eradicate the sheen!).

❖ Keep chocolate away from light, for example, by storing it in a box.

❖ Keep handling to a minimum.

HOW TO HANDLE CHOCOLATES

Obviously, you can ignore the following if your main concern is keeping the time it takes to get your chocolate from the cooking bowl into your mouth to a minimum and presentation is not a priority!

❖ Keep handling to a minimum: chocolate marks and scratches very easily.

❖ Try not to handle the chocolate while it is warm (such as just after it has been coated).

❖ The cooler your hands the better. If you are particularly warm-blooded, try cooling your hands under running cold water (but thoroughly dry your hands afterwards), or, even, leave them in the freezer for as long as you can bear!

❖ Gloves can be useful, especially if they are concealing fingers which have visited places the environmental health officer would rather not know about! However, ensure the gloves are cleaned or wiped frequently, since, unlike when using bare hands, you cannot feel the greasy residues which accumulate from handling the chocolates.

HOW TO TRANSPORT YOUR WORKS OF ART

If I was playing at word associations and 'transport' came up, I would have to follow it with 'apoplexy', since there have been so many occasions when getting my wares from A to B has proved the most problematical part of chocolate-making.

❖ Chocolate-battering is a very worrying scourge, and common sense should prevail as to how the chocolate items should be packaged, corresponding to how rough the handling is expected to be. If a rough road is to be expected, such as a lorry failing to avoid potholes, it is essential that the chocolates cannot move around within the packaging. However, I have not, as yet, come across a fail-safe technique against the delivery man who decides to improve on his rugby passing-skills with your work of art. 'Fragile' plastered all over the box only seems to encourage him!

HEAT

❖ This is a major problem as our climate continues to change and our warm seasons appear to get longer and hotter. Cool boxes can be very effective as a countermeasure backed up, if necessary, by one or more icepacks, wrapped in towelling and not placed in direct contact with the chocolates. In the absence of cool boxes, placing your box of chocolates within one or more boxes, using scrumpled up newspaper as an insulator, can help to stave off the heat. If you are leaving chocolates in your car, try to park in the shade or, preferably, take them with you, since chocolate can melt distressingly quickly.

HOW TO GET THE MOST OUT OF EATING YOUR CHOCOLATE

If I allowed myself to be flippant, I would simply say 'Stick it in your mouth', but the following serious points are worth considering:

❖ The temperature of your ganache-filled chocolate is very important when it comes to getting the most pleasure out of it. Too cold, such as straight out of the refrigerator, and the subtleties and strength of some of the flavours will be missed. Too warm and the ganache can taste disappointingly greasy and will seem to be of a rough, cloying texture. Personally, I feel the best temperature is if the chocolate is at around 18°C.

❖ If you need to have a clean, unadulterated palate, for example if you are conducting a comparison-tasting of several different makes or flavours, instead of sipping sparkling water between each tasting you might find a slice of apple surprisingly cleansing.

❖ Avoid going for the chocolate of the same flavour that you are eating or drinking. For example, the taste of a coffee-flavoured chocolate is lost when drinking coffee.

❖ The amount of time for which you let your chocolate linger around the tastebuds before you send it packing down the oesophagus can affect what you taste. If, at the sight of a chocolate on a plate, you are used to grabbing the whole chocolate, shoving it in your mouth, and dispatching it to the stomach before you have time to blink, try consciously biting half the chocolate first. As with wine-tasting, swill it around the mouth for a few seconds and you may well experience a whole range of tastes which you might otherwise have missed. Unlike with wine, you do not need to spit it out!

WHAT TO DO WITH LEFTOVER GANACHE

❖ Ganache freezes well. In fact, some improve with freezing. However, ensure that all surfaces are covered, because they may dry out from freezer burn. Food bags are good for this purpose.

❖ Ganache can be used for making an unusually flavoured and rich hot chocolate drink. Add around two tablespoons of ganache and one to two teaspoons of cocoa powder to a saucepan containing a mugful of boiling milk and mix thoroughly, preferably using a whisk but a spoon or spatula will suffice, until all the chocolate has melted. For a wickedly rich but heavenly concoction, replace around a third of the milk with double cream.

❖ If you add more cream, you can use ganache as a filling for a cake or as the chocolate flavouring for an ice cream.

WHAT TO DO WITH LEFTOVER CHOCOLATE (WITHOUT ANY GANACHE)

❖ Any remaining tempered chocolate can, very conveniently, be used again at a later date. However, each time you temper it, it will get slightly thicker, and so I suggest that you add at least the same amount of fresh chocolate to it, when you next come to use it for coating or moulding work.

❖ Any failures, mishaps or creations you do not wish others to see can be returned to the melting pot, leaving behind no trace of their existence!

❖ Eat it!

HOW TO CARE FOR YOUR MOULDS

If you wish to get a lot of use out of your moulds, the following precautions are important, since any scratches or marks on the inside will show up on your works of art.

❖ When not in use, store the moulds upside-down, at room temperature should be fine.

❖ Try not to handle the inside of the moulds: finger nails can easily scratch and fingerprints will be relocated to the finished article.

❖ Although moulds can be washed, keep washing to a minimum since, no matter how careful you are, very small scratches will appear.

❖ When washing, use warm water (up to 50°C), with a small amount of mild washing-up liquid; hot water can damage the moulds. Use a soft cloth or non-abrasive sponge to remove any stubborn stains by rubbing gently.

❖ When drying your moulds, do not leave them to drip dry; this can leave water marks, which will transfer themselves to your otherwise gleaming finished product. Rather, use cotton wool or soft tissue paper.

❖ Instead of washing moulds with water, an alternative way of cleaning them, if the stains are purely chocolate in origin, is to fill the dirty mould with just one type of tempered chocolate and allow it to set. When the set chocolate is removed from the mould, it should take with it all the unwanted

blemishes, leaving behind a sparkling clean mould (on the inside, anyway!).

❖ Another 'dry' method is to heat the moulds gently with a hair dryer and then wipe off the oily residue with cotton wool or soft tissue paper.

How to clean up

Am I preaching to the converted? Probably not, since the following tips demonstrate that chocolate seems to have its own set of rules.

❖ When washing, chocolate can be stubborn right to the end, clinging on to anything it can grab hold of until there is nowhere to go other than down the plug-hole! With the exception of moulds, water should be as hot as possible (washing-up gloves are appreciated) and lavish amounts of washing-up liquid are needed. Chocolate will not disappear of its own accord and will need to be helped on its way by a combination of a brush (small ones like those used for cleaning baby bottles are useful for those nooks and crannies) a rough sponge and running hot water.

❖ Rinsing in hot, clean water should ensure the removal of any lingering cocoa butter, which is invisible when wet but, when dry, can give utensils the appearance of never having been near a bowl of water!

❖ Before consigning the dirty utensils to the sink, try removing as much chocolate as possible, which is done more easily if the chocolate is still warm or soft. If not, you may be surprised by how quickly a small amount of chocolate will dirty your water.

❖ Chocolate on the floor can be washed away by using plenty of elbow grease and hot water. The task is easier if you first scrape up any lumps of chocolate, using a scraper, the rim of a dustpan or the edge of a broom or brush.

❖ Chocolate on work surfaces can be dealt with in the same way, although you may not wish to use the dustpan or broom. If you do not wish to use water (for example, you have bowls of chocolate around which must not be splashed), get out your hair dryer and wipe away the warmed lumps using a damp rag.

❖ Chocolate on your clothes, especially your chicest outfit, gives good cause to curse, for chocolate does not wash off well. Immediately remove as much as you can with a clean, damp, warm cloth before the chocolate sets. The residual brownish oil stain will eventually disappear with repeated cleaning. I have not found soaking in bleach to be useful.

❖ Chocolate under the finger nails, especially if your nails are otherwise diligently manicured, can be an unwelcome sight. A long, relaxing and painless soak in the bath is more effective than using a nailbrush and running hot water.

How to stay clean

After having read the preceding section, which could have been given the subtitle 'The nightmare of chocolate!', keeping as clean as possible en route in the long run is the best strategy.

❖ Wipe up any spills before they set: chocolate is easier to clean when still soft. A cloth permanently near at hand is a blessing.

❖ Keep the floor as clean as possible: chocolate readily adheres to the soles of your shoes and is happy to be transported round the house to your most valuable carpet!

❖ Wear an apron, avoid wearing your smartest clothes and roll up your sleeves.

❖ Turn on the answerphone! If you do have to answer the phone (or for that matter turn on a light or open a door) when coated in chocolate, grab hold of a cloth and ensure that it remains between you and the immaculate surface.

❖ When using cocoa powder, close your windows, cover nearby areas and avoid sneezing! Cocoa powder is very adept at travelling!

❖ Before going out, always look at yourself in the mirror first! You may be surprised by where the chocolate has managed to nestle without your knowing.

Directory

The character of the British chocolate market is changing rapidly, as witnessed by the increasing interest in chocolate with a high mass of cocoa solids, and by the growth of small chocolate specialists. Therefore, despite having made every effort to ensure the following is as helpful and as up-to-date as possible, I apologise in advance if these rapid changes have meant that I have omitted certain individuals or companies, or if details correct at the time of writing are now obsolete. However, if you encounter any problems or wish to be updated, please feel welcome to contact me care of Boxtree, Macmillan Publishers, 25 Eccleston Place, London SW1W 9NF.

SUPPLIERS OF CHOCOLATE/*COUVERTURE*

While chocolate is of course very widely available, it is harder to find more specialist types such as *couverture*.

Mainstream supermarkets: their range is, I am pleased to report, increasing as is generally the quality, although I do advise you to shop around since quality is not consistent. You may even find *couverture*, but confusingly it will probably be labelled as cooking chocolate. However, it is unlikely that you will find 100% cocoa mass.

Department stores and specialist shops: here you are more likely to find a wider selection of chocolate for coating and cooking purposes. The following are specially recommended, and will probably stock 100% cocoa mass:

LONDON
The Chocolate Society Shop,
36 Elizabeth Street,
London SW1W 9NZ
(tel. 0171 259 9222).
Also sells coloured couverture and other chocolate-related products.
For mail order, apply to
The Chocolate Society,
Clay Pit Lane, Roecliffe,
North Yorkshire YO5 9LS
(tel. 01423 322230)

Rococo (run by Chantal Coady),
321 Kings Road,
London SW3 5EP
(tel. 0171 352 5857)

Theobroma Chocolates,
93 West Yard,
Camden Lock Place,
Chalk Farm Road,
London NW1 8AF
(tel. 0171 284 2670)

Villandry,
89 Marylebone High Street,
London W1M 3DE
(tel. 0171 487 3816)

SOUTH
Montgomery Moore,
17 Tunsgate, Guildford,
Surrey GU1 3QT
(tel. 01483 451620)

WEST
Waterman's Foodhall,
142 Whiteladies Road,
Clifton, Bristol BS8 2RS
(tel. 0117 973 2846)

Melchior,
Station Road,
South Molton, Devon
EX36 3LL
(tel. 01769 574442)

NORTH
Hannah's (run by Tom Phillips),
Chocolate and Sugarcraft Shop,
10 Barrow Road, Quorn,
Leicestershire LE12 8DL
(tel. 01509 416638)

Comestibles,
82 Bailgate, Lincoln LN1 3AR
(tel. 01522 520010)

SCOTLAND
The Cake & Chocolate Shop,
12 Bruntsfield Place, Edinburgh
EH10 4HN
(tel. 0131 228 4350)
Also sells colouring for chocolate

The Finishing Touch,
17 Saint Patrick Square,
Edinburgh EH8 9EZ
(tel. 0131 667 0914)
Also sells basic equipment, as well as colourings and books

The Harvest Garden,
58 Morningside Road,
Edinburgh EH10 4BZ
(tel. 0131 447 1788)

Valvona & Crolla,
19 Elm Road,
Edinburgh EH7 4AA
(tel. 0131 556 6066)
Also stocks some moulds and basic equipment

Suppliers to the trade/mail order: these normally supply in bulk, but the following will probably deliver, although you may have to collect yourself or there may be a minimum delivery; their policies can have a tendency of changing rapidly. However, a quick telephone call should put you in the picture.

V Benoist Ltd,
8-10 Eldon Way,
London NW10 7QX
(tel. 0181 965 9531) supply all types of *couverture* as well as coloured chocolate and other products

Keylink Ltd,
Blackburn Road,
Rotherham S61 2DR, S Yorks
(tel. 01709 550206) are happy to supply both the individual and businesses with a large and varied range of products, and also supply coloured pigment

Lakes Food Euro Ltd,
Cumberland Park,
26-100 Scrubs Lane,
London NW10 6AH
(tel. 0181 968 0261)

Leathams Larder,
114 Camberwell Road,
London SE5 0EE
(tel. 0171 703 7031) supply all types of *couverture* as well as colouring for chocolate and other chocolate-related products

Vin Sullivan Foods Ltd,
Gilchrist Thomas,
Blaenavon, Gwent NP4 9RL
(tel. 01495 792792)

EQUIPMENT

Including moulds, decorating forks and sometimes more expensive equipment such as coating machines or tempering kettles. Some specialist catering retailers may stock a limited range of products.

Continental Chefs Suppliers
(*mail order only*),
Unit 4,
South Hetton Industrial Estate,
County Durham DH6 2UZ
(tel. 0191 526 4107)

Keylink Ltd,
Blackburn Road,
Rotherham S61 2DR, S Yorks
(tel. 01709 550206) supply a large range of equipment and books

Nisbets (*mail order*),
1110 Aztec West,
Bristol BS2 4HR
(tel. 01454 855555)

Norman Bartleet, Lion House,
Petersfield Avenue, Slough,
Berkshire SL2 5DN
(tel. 01753 822171) supply a large range of moulds and also supply coating/enrobing equipment

Squires Kitchen Sugarcraft,
Squires House,
3 Waverley Lane,
Farnham, Surrey GU9 8BB
(tel. 01252 711749) supply a good range of chocolate equipment and literature geared towards home chocolate making

Vantage House,
Unit 4,
38-42 Brunswick Street, Brighton,
E Sussex BN3 1EL
(tel. 01273 749000) supply a range of specialist chocolate equipment

Vin Sullivan Foods Ltd,
Gilchrist Thomas,
Blaenavon, Gwent NP4 9RL
(tel. 01495 792792)

FURTHER ADVICE AND INFORMATION

Couverture suppliers
Because these are normally linked to buying couverture in bulk, these usually cater for professionals:

Cacao Barry, who can be contacted care of V Benoist Ltd (opposite), and Vin Sullivan Foods Ltd (opposite)

Lesmie-Callebaut, Wildmere Industrial Estate, Banbury, OX16 7UU (tel. 01295 257651)

Teaching colleges
These tend to be geared towards the catering professional, although you might be able to persuade them otherwise!

Thomas Danby College, Roundhay Road, Leeds LS7 3BG (tel. 01132 494912)

Westminster College, 76 Vincent Square, London SW1 2PD (tel. 0171 626 1222) organises one-day courses for the public and professionals alike, as well as longer courses

L'Ecole LeNotre, 40 Rue Pierre Curie, B.P.6, 78373 Plaisir Cedex, France (tel. 00331 30 61 46 34) is an example of a well-run training centre which is tagged onto a large manufacturing site, providing various courses for different levels.

Courses for the general public
These unfortunately seem to be far-flung, but they are on the increase:

Hannah's *(Tom Phillips)*, Chocolate and Sugarcraft Shop, 10 Barrow Road, Quorn, Leicestershire LE12 8DL (tel. 01509 416638)

Melchior *(Carlo Melchior)*, Station Road, South Molton, Devon EX36 3LL (tel. 01769 574442)

Special Edition Continental Chocolate *(Scotty Scot)*, Honeyholes Lane, Dunholme, Lincolnshire LN2 3SU (tel. 01673 860616)

Squires Kitchen Sugarcraft, Squires House, 3 Waverley Lane, Farnham, Surrey GU9 8BB (tel. 01252 711749)

For further information, outings, tastings or advice try the following enthusiasts:

Cadbury Ltd, P.O. Box 12, Bournville, Birmingham B30 2LU (tel. 0121 458 2000) Information packs available, as well as visits to their museum and factory

Chocolate Society, Clay Pit Lane, Roecliffe, North Yorkshire YO5 9LS (tel. 01423 322230) Arranges tastings, produces a newsletter, and can give technical advice

Chocoholics Unanimous (tel. 01656 786992) A small, self-funding group of chocolate passionees who arrange opportunities to further their enjoyment, such as tastings, visits to factories, or meals centred around chocolate

Mars Confectionery, Dundee Road, Slough, SL1 4JX (tel. 01753 550055)

Terry Suchard, St George's House, Bayshill Road, Cheltenham, Gloucestershire GL50 3AE